Crime and **Punishments**

Including a New Translation of Beccaria's 'Dei Delitti e delle Pene'

MAVEN BOOKS

Crime and **Punishments**

Including a New Translation of Beccaria's 'Dei Delitti e delle Pene'

James Anson Farrer

MAVEN BOOKS

MAVEN BOOKS

An Imprint of **MJP Publishers**

ISBN 9789355278241

MAVEN Books
No. 44, Nallathambi Street,
Triplicane, Chennai 600 005

Printed and bound in India

MJP 1676

Publisher : C. Janarthanan

PREFACE

The reason for translating afresh Beccaria's 'Dei Delitti e delle Pene' ('Crimes and Punishments') is, that it is a classical work of its kind, and that the interest which belongs to it is still far from being merely historical.

It was translated into English long ago; but the change in the order of the several chapters and paragraphs, which the work underwent before it was clothed in its final dress, is so great, that the new translation and the old one really constitute quite different books.

The object of the preliminary chapters is to place the historical importance of the original in its just light, and to increase the interest of the subjects it discusses.

The Translator has abstained from all criticism or comment of the original, less from complete agreement with all its ideas than from the conviction that annotations are more often vexatious than profitable, and are best left to the reader to make for himself. There is scarcely a sentence in the book on which a commentator might not be prolix.

To combine the maximum of perspicuity with the maximum of fidelity to the original has been the cardinal principle observed in the translation. But it would, of course, have been no less impossible than contrary to the spirit of the original to have attempted to render perfectly comprehensible what the author purposely wrapped in obscurity. A translation can but follow the lights and shades of the surface it reflects, rendering clear what is clear in the original, and opaque what is opaque.

'All men, whether singly or collectively, naturally do wrong, nor is there any law which will prevent it. For every kind of punishment has been successively tried by mankind, if haply they might suffer less injury from malefactors. And it is probable that in their origin punishments for even the gravest crimes are comparatively mild, but that, as they are disregarded, most of them come in course of time to be punishments of death; yet this in its turn is also disregarded. Either, therefore, some greater terror than death must be invented, or death at least serves not as a deterrent, men being led to risk it, sometimes by poverty, which emboldens them through necessity, sometimes by power, which makes them overreaching and insolent; or sometimes by some other circumstance which subordinates all a man's passions to some one passion that is insuperable and dominant.... And it is simply impossible, and a very foolish idea, to think that, when human nature is firmly bent on doing anything, it can be deterred from it either by force of law or by any other terror.'—THUCYDIDES.

'How many condemnations have I seen more criminal than the crimes themselves!'—MONTAIGNE.

CONTENTS

CHAPTER I

Beccaria's Life And Character

The 'Dei Delitti e delle Pene' was published for the first time in 1764. It quickly ran through several editions, and was first translated into French in 1766 by the Abbé Morellet, since which time it has been translated into most of the languages of Europe, not excluding Greek and Russian.

The author of the book was a native of Milan, then part of the Austrian dominions, and under the governorship of Count Firmian, a worthy representative of the liberal despotism of Maria Theresa and her chief minister, Kaunitz. Under Firmian's administration a period of beneficial reforms began for Lombardy. Agriculture was encouraged, museums and libraries extended, great works of public utility carried on. Even the Church was shorn of her privileges, and before Firmian had been ten years in Lombardy all traces of ecclesiastical immunity had been destroyed; the jurisdiction of the Church, and her power to hold lands in mortmain were restricted, the right of asylum was abolished, and, above all, the Holy Office of the Inquisition. Let these few facts suffice to indicate the spirit of the immediate political surroundings in the midst of which Beccaria's work appeared.

But, in spite of the liberalism of the Count, the penal laws and customs of Lombardy remained the same; and the cruel legal procedure by torture existed still, untouched by the salutary reforms effected in other departments of the Government. There was the preparatory torture, to extort confession from criminals not yet condemned; there was torture for the discovery of a criminal's accomplices; and there was the extraordinary or greater torture, which preceded the execution of a sentence of death. It is true that torture could only be applied to crimes of a capital nature, but there was scarcely an act in the possible category of crimes that was not then punishable with death. Proofs of guilt were sought almost entirely from torture and secret accusations, whilst penalties depended less on the text of any known law than on the discretion—that is, on the caprice—of the magistrate.

It was this system that Beccaria's little work destroyed, and had that been its only result, it would still deserve to live in men's memories for its historical interest alone. For upon the legislation of that time, and especially upon that of Italy, this pamphlet on criminal law broke like a ray of sunlight on a dungeon floor, making even blacker that which was black before by the very brilliancy which it shed upon it. To Beccaria primarily, though not of course solely, belongs the glory of having expelled the use of torture from every legal tribunal throughout Christendom.

Frederick the Great had already abolished it in Prussia;[1] it had been discontinued in Sweden; it was not recognised in the military codes of Europe, and Beccaria said it was not in use in England. This was true generally, although the *peine forte et dure*, by which a prisoner who would not plead was subjected to be squeezed nearly to death by an iron weight, was not abolished till the year 1771.[2]

It is remarkable that a book which has done more for law reform than any other before or since should have been written by a man who was not a lawyer by profession, who was totally unversed in legal practice, and who was only twenty-six when he attacked a system of law which had on its side all authority, living and dead. Hume was not twenty-seven when he published his 'Treatise on Human Nature,' nor was Berkeley more than twenty-six when he published his 'Principles of Human Knowledge.' The similar precocity displayed by Beccaria is suggestive, therefore, of the inquiry, how far the greatest revolutions in the thoughts or customs of the world have been due to writers under thirty years of age.

The following letter by Beccaria to the Abbé Morellet in acknowledgment of the latter's translation of his treatise is perhaps the best introduction to the life and character of the author. The letter in question has been quoted by Villemain in proof of the debt owed by the Italian literature of the last century to that of France, but from the allusions therein contained to Hume and the 'Spectator' it is evident that something also was due to our own. Beccaria had spent eight years of his youth in the college of the Jesuits at Parma, with what sense of gratitude this letter will show. The following is a translation of the greater part of it:—

Your letter has raised in me sentiments of the deepest esteem, of the greatest gratitude, and the most tender friendship; nor can I confess to you

1 By a Cabinet Order of June 3, 1740. See Carlyle's *Frederick the Great*, iii. 7.

2 Pike, *History of Crime in England*, ii. 283, 346.

how honoured I feel at seeing my work translated into the language of a nation which is the mistress and illuminator of Europe. I owe everything to French books. They first raised in my mind feelings of humanity which had been suffocated by eight years of a fanatical education. I cannot express to you the pleasure with which I have read your translation; you have embellished the original, and your arrangement seems more natural than, and preferable to, my own. You had no need to fear offending the author's vanity: in the first place, because a book that treats of the cause of humanity belongs, when once published, to the world and all nations equally; and as to myself in particular, I should have made little progress in the philosophy of the heart, which I place above that of the intellect, had I not acquired the courage to see and love the truth. I hope that the fifth edition, which will appear shortly, will be soon exhausted, and I assure you that in the sixth I will follow entirely, or nearly so, the arrangement of your translation, which places the truth in a better light than I have sought to place it in.

As to the obscurity you find in the work, I heard, as I wrote, the clash of chains that superstition still shakes, and the cries of fanaticism that drown the voice of truth; and the perception of this frightful spectacle induced me sometimes to veil the truth in clouds. I wished to defend truth, without making myself her martyr. This idea of the necessity of obscurity has made me obscure sometimes without necessity. Add to this my inexperience and my want of practice in writing, pardonable in an author of twenty-eight,[3] who only five years ago first set foot in the career of letters.

D'Alembert, Diderot, Helvetius, Buffon, Hume, illustrious names, which no one can hear without emotion! Your immortal works are my continual study, the object of my occupation by day, of my meditation in the silence of night. Full of the truth which you teach, how could I ever have burned incense to worshipped error, or debased myself to lie to posterity? I find myself rewarded beyond my hopes in the signs of esteem I have received from these celebrated persons, my masters. Convey to each of these, I pray you, my most humble thanks, and assure them that I feel for them that profound and true respect which a feeling soul entertains for truth and virtue.

---

3 Beccaria was born in 1738, and his book appeared in 1764. Therefore he was only 26. The 28 must refer to the time he wrote the letter.

My occupation is to cultivate philosophy in peace, and so to satisfy my three strongest passions, the love, that is, of literary fame, the love of liberty, and pity for the ills of mankind, slaves of so many errors. My conversion to philosophy only dates back five years, and I owe it to my perusal of the 'Lettres Persanes.' The second work that completed my mental revolution was that of Helvetius. The latter forced me irresistibly into the way of truth, and aroused my attention for the first time to the blindness and miseries of humanity.

... I lead a tranquil and solitary life, if a select company of friends in which the heart and mind are in continual movement can be called solitude. This is my consolation, and prevents me feeling in my own country as if I were in exile.

My country is quite immersed in prejudices, left in it by its ancient masters. The Milanese have no pardon for those who would have them live in the eighteenth century. In a capital which counts 120,000 inhabitants, you will scarcely find twenty who love to instruct themselves, and who sacrifice to truth and virtue. My friends and I, persuaded that periodical works are among the best means for tempting to some sort of reading minds incapable of more serious application, are publishing in papers, after the manner of the English 'Spectator,' a work which in England has contributed so much to increase mental culture and the progress of good sense. The French philosophers have a colony in this America, and we are their disciples because we are the disciples of reason, &c.

Thus, the two writers to whom Beccaria owed most were Montesquieu and Helvetius. The 'Lettres Persanes' of the former, which satirised so many things then in custom, contained but little about penal laws; but the idea is there started for the first time that crimes depend but little on the mildness or severity of the punishments attached to them. 'The imagination,' says the writer, 'bends of itself to the customs of the country; and eight days of prison or a slight fine have as much terror for a European brought up in a country of mild manners as the loss of an arm would have for an Asiatic.'[4] The 'Esprit des Lois,' by the same author, probably contributed more to the formation of Beccaria's thoughts than the 'Lettres Persanes,' for it is impossible to read the twelfth book of that work without being struck by the resemblance of ideas. The 'De L'Esprit' of Helvetius was condemned by the Sorbonne as 'a combination of all the various kinds of poison scattered through modern

4 *Lettre 80.*

books.' Yet it was one of the most influential books of the time. We find Hume recommending it to Adam Smith for its agreeable composition father than for its philosophy; and a writer who had much in common with Beccaria drew from it the same inspiration that he did. That writer was Bentham, who tells us that when he was about twenty, and on a visit to his father and stepmother in the country, he would often walk behind them reading a book, and that his favourite author was Helvetius.

The influence of the predominant French philosophy appears throughout Beccaria's treatise. Human justice is based on the idea of public utility, and the object of legislation is to conduct men to the greatest possible happiness or to the least possible misery. The vein of dissatisfaction with life and of disbelief in human virtue is a marked feature of Beccaria's philosophy. To him life is a desert, in which a few physical pleasures lie scattered here and there;[5] his own country is only a place of exile, save for the presence of a few friends engaged like himself in a war with ignorance. Human ideas of morality and virtue have only been produced in the course of many centuries and after much bloodshed, but slow and difficult as their growth has been, they are ever ready to disappear at the slightest breeze that blows against them.

Beccaria entertains a similar despair of truth. The history of mankind represents a vast sea of errors, in which at rare intervals a few truths only float uppermost; and the durability of great truths is as that of a flash of lightning when compared with the long and dark night which envelops humanity. For this reason he is ready to be the servant of truth, not her martyr; and he recommends in the search for truth, as in the other affairs of life, a little of that 'philosophical indolence' which cares not too much about results, and which a writer like Montaigne is best fitted to inspire.[6]

The few select friends who made life at Milan just supportable were Pietro and Alessandro Verri, Frisi, and some others. Pietro Verri was ten years older than Beccaria, and it was at his instance that the latter wrote his first treatise on a subject which then demanded some attention, namely, 'The Disorders and Remedies of the Coinage.' This work was published two years before the 'Crimes and Punishments,' but though it provoked much discussion at the time, it has long since ceased to have any interest.

5 *I Piaceri della Immaginazione*, in his collected works by Villari, p. 546.

6 Villari, *Opere di Beccaria*, 547.

Count Pietro Verri was the son of Gabriel, who was distinguished alike for his legal knowledge and high position in Milan. At the house of Pietro, Beccaria and the other friends used to meet for the discussion and study of political and social questions. Alessandro, the younger brother of Pietro, held the office of 'Protector of Prisoners,' an office which consisted in visiting the prisons, listening to the grievances of the inmates, and discovering, if possible, reasons for their defence or for mercy. The distressing sights he was witness of in this capacity are said to have had the most marked effect upon him; and there is no doubt that this fact caused the attention of the friends to be so much directed to the state of the penal laws. It is believed to have been at the instigation of the two brothers that Beccaria undertook the work which was destined to make his name so famous.

Why then did Pietro Verri not write it himself? The answer would seem to be, out of deference for the position and opinions of his father. It was some time later that Gabriel defended the use of torture in the Milanese Senate, and Pietro wrote a work on torture which he did not publish in his father's lifetime. It was probably due also to the father's position that Alessandro held his office of Protector of the Prisoners, so that there were obvious reasons which prevented either brother from undertaking the work in question.

It was at one time said that the work really was Pietro Verri's and not Beccaria's, for it was published anonymously, and away from Milan. The domestic circumstances of Pietro lent some countenance to this story, as did also the fact that he charged himself with the trouble of making a correct copy of the manuscript, so that a copy of the treatise does actually exist in Pietro's handwriting. The story, however, has long since been disproved; yet to show the great interest which Pietro took in the work, and the ready assistance he gave to his friend, a letter to him from Beccaria, with respect to the second edition, deserves mention, in which Beccaria begs him not only to revise the spelling correctly, but generally to erase, add, and correct, as he pleases. It would appear that he was already tired of literary success, for he tells his friend, that but for the motive of preserving his esteem and of affording fresh aliment to their friendship, he should from indolence prefer obscurity to glory itself.

There is no doubt that Beccaria always had a strong preference for the contemplative as opposed to the practical and active life, and that but for his friend Pietro Verri he would probably never have distinguished himself at all. He would have said with Plato that a wise man should regard life as a storm, and hide himself behind a wall till it be overpast. He almost does say this in his essay on the 'Pleasures of the Imagination,' published soon after the 'Crimes and Punishments.' He advises his reader to stand aside and look on at the rest of mankind as they run about in their blind confusion; to make his relations with them as few as possible; and if he will do them any good, to do it at that distance which will prevent them from upsetting him or drawing him away in their own vortex. Let him in happy contemplation enjoy in silence the few moments that separate his birth from his disappearance. Let him leave men to fight, to hope, and to die; and with a smile both at himself and at them, let him repose softly on that enlightened indifference with regard to human things which will not deprive him of the pleasure of being just and beneficent, but which will spare him from those useless troubles and changes from evil to good that vex the greater part of mankind.

This essay on the 'Imagination' was published soon after the 'Crimes and Punishments' in the periodical to which Beccaria alludes in his letter to Morellet. 'The Caffè' was the name of the periodical which, from June 1764, he and his friends published every tenth day for a period of two years. The model of the paper was the English 'Spectator,' and its object to propagate useful knowledge pleasantly among the Milanese, whilst its name rested on the supposition that the friends who composed it executed their labours during meetings in a coffee-house. The most interesting contributions to it by Beccaria are his 'Fragment on Style,' his article on 'Periodical Newspapers,' and his essay on the 'Pleasures of the Imagination.'

The publication of the 'Delitti e delle Pene' interrupted its author's dreams of philosophical calm, by fulfilling his hopes of literary fame. The French encyclopædists were the first to recognise its merits, and D'Alembert, the mathematician, at once predicted for the writer the reward of an immortal reputation. Morellet's translation, in which the arrangement, though not the matter of the text, was entirely altered, ran through seven editions in six months, and Beccaria, as has been seen, was only too delighted with the honour thus conferred on him to complain in any way of the liberties taken by the translator with the original.

A still greater honour was the commentary written by Voltaire. The fact that only within a few miles of his own residence a girl of eighteen had been hung for the exposure of a bastard child led Voltaire to welcome Beccaria's work as a sign that a period of softer manners and more humane laws was about to dawn upon the world's history. Should not a people, he argues, who like the French pique themselves on their politeness also pride themselves on their humanity? Should they retain the use of torture, merely because it was an ancient custom, when the experience of England and other countries showed that crimes were not more numerous in countries where it was not in use, and when reason indicated the absurdity of inflicting on a man, before his condemnation, a punishment more horrible than would await his proved guilt? What could be more cruel, too, than the maxim of law that a man who forfeited his life forfeited his estates? What more inhuman than thus to punish a whole family for the crime of an individual, perhaps condemning a wife and children to beg their bread because the head of the family had harboured a Protestant preacher or listened to his sermon in a cavern or a desert? Amid the contrariety of laws that governed France, the object of the criminal procedure to bring an accused man to destruction might be said to be the only law which was uniform throughout the country.

So signal a success in France was a sufficient guarantee of success elsewhere. A knowledge of the book must have speedily crossed the Channel, for Blackstone quoted it the very year after its publication. It was first translated into English in 1768, together with Voltaire's commentary; but just as Morellet's translation professed to have been published at Philadelphia, so the English translator kept his name a secret. The Economical Society of Berne, which was accustomed to bestow a gold medal on the writer of the best treatise on any given subject, violated its own rules in favour of the anonymous writer of the 'Delitti,' inviting him to disclose his name, and to accept the gold medal 'as a sign of esteem due to a citizen who had dared to raise his voice in favour of humanity against the most deeply engrained prejudices.'

But there was another side to the brightness of this success. In literature as in war no position of honour can be won or held without danger, and of this Beccaria seems to have been conscious when he pleaded against the charge of obscurity, that in writing he had had before his eyes the fear of ecclesiastical persecution. His love for truth, he confessed, stopped short at the risk of martyrdom. He had, indeed, three very clear warnings to justify his fears. Muratori, the historian, had suffered much from accusations of heresy and atheism, and had owed his immunity from worse consequences chiefly to the liberal protection of Pope Benedict XIV. The Marquis Scipio Maffei had also incurred similar charges for his historical handling of the subject of Free-will. But there was even a stronger warning than these, and one not likely to be lost on a man with youth and life before him; that was the fate of the unfortunate Giannone, who, only sixteen years before Beccaria wrote, had ended with his life in the citadel of Turin an imprisonment that had lasted twenty years, for certain observations on the Church of Rome which he had been rash enough to insert in his 'History of Naples.'

Of all the attacks which the publication of the 'Dei Delitti' provoked, the bitterest came naturally from a theological pen. At the very time that Beccaria's work appeared, the Republic of Venice was occupied in a violent contest touching the Inquisitorial Council of Ten; and imagining that Beccaria's remarks about secret accusations had been directed against the procedure of their famous tribunal, whilst they attributed the work to a Venetian nobleman called Quirini, they forbade its circulation under pain of death. It was on their behalf and with this belief that the Dominican Padre, Facchinei, took up his pen and wrote a book, entitled, 'Notes and Observations on the "Dei Delitti,"' in which he argued, among other things, not only that secret accusations were the best, cheapest, and most effective method of carrying out justice, but that torture was a kind of mercy to a criminal, purging him in his death from the sin of falsehood.

In these 'Notes and Observations' Beccaria and his work were assailed with that vigour and lucidity for which the Dominican school of writing has always been so conspicuous. The author was described as 'a man of narrow mind,' 'a madman,' 'a stupid impostor,' 'full of poisonous bitterness and calumnious mordacity.' He was accused of writing 'with sacrilegious imposture against the Inquisition,' of believing that 'religion was incompatible with the good government of a state;' nay, he was condemned 'by all the reasonable world as the enemy of Christianity, a bad philosopher, and a bad man.' His book was stigmatised as 'sprung from the deepest abyss of darkness, horrible, monstrous, full of poison,' containing 'miserable arguments,' 'insolent blasphemies,' and so forth.

This fulmination reached Milan on January 15, 1765, and on the 21st the Risposta, or reply, was ready for publication.[7] This defence was the work of his friends, the Verris, and was published, like the original, anonymously; as it was written in the first person throughout, it was generally at the time and even till lately ascribed to the same author as the original, but the fact is now established beyond doubt that the real

7 It is published in the Haarlem edition of the *Dei Delitti*, 1766.

authors were Pietro and his brother. The writers wisely refrained from the use of retaliatory language, confining themselves in their defence solely to charges of irreligion and sedition, responding to six which accused Beccaria of the latter, and to twenty-three which declared him guilty of the former.

But it is probable that Beccaria owed his escape from persecution less to his apology than to the liberal protection of Count Firmian, who in his report of the affair to the Court of Vienna spoke of the Risposta as 'full of moderation and honourable to the character of its author.' That the Count fully agreed with Beccaria's opinions on torture is proved by a letter he wrote, in which he declares himself to have been much pleased with what Beccaria had said on the subject. His vanity, he said, had been flattered by it, for his own feelings about torture had always been the same. The book seemed to him written with much love of humanity and much imagination. Beccaria always acknowledged his gratitude to the Count for his action in this matter. To Morellet he wrote, that he owed the Count his tranquillity, in having protected his book; and when, a few years later, he published his book on Style, he dedicated it to Firmian as his benefactor, thanking him for having scattered the clouds that envy and ignorance had gathered thickly over his head, and for having protected one whose only object had been to declare with the greatest caution and respect the interests of humanity.

Less dangerous personally than the theological criticism, but more pernicious to reform, was the hostile criticism that at once appeared from the thick phalanx of professional lawyers, the sound-thinking 'practical men.' From whom only two short extracts need be rescued from oblivion, as illustrations of the objections once raised against ideas which have since become the common groundwork of all subsequent legislation, in America as well as in Europe. The first extract is from a work on criminal justice by a lawyer of Provence, who in 1770 wrote as follows:—

The treatise 'Dei Delitti,' instead of throwing any light on the subject of crimes, or on the manner in which they should be punished, tends to establish a system of the most dangerous and novel ideas, which, if adopted, would go so far as to overturn laws received hitherto by the greater part of all civilised nations.

And an advocate to the Parliament of Paris thus expressed himself, in refutation of Beccaria:—

What can be thought of an author who presumes to establish his system on the *débris* of all hitherto accepted notions, who to accredit it condemns all civilised nations, and who spares neither systems of law, nor magistrates, nor lawyers?

But of far greater historical interest than such criticism is that of Ramsay, the Scotch poet and painter, to whom a copy of Beccaria's treatise had been shown by Diderot, and who wrote a letter about it to the latter, which, though it contains some very just criticisms on Beccaria, yet reads for the most part very curiously by the light of subsequent history, and illustrates graphically the despair of all reform then felt by most men of reflection.[8]

Ramsay argues that the penal laws of a particular country can only be considered with reference to the needs of a particular country, and not in the abstract; that the government of a country will always enforce laws with a view to its own security; and that nothing less than a general revolution will ever make the holders of political power listen for a moment to the claims of philosophers.

But (he goes on) since it would be an absurd folly to expect this general revolution, this general reconstruction, which could only be effected by very violent means, such as would be at least a very great misfortune for the present generation, and hold out an uncertain prospect of compensation for the next one, every speculative work, like the 'Dei Delitti e delle Pene,' enters into the category of Utopias, of Platonic Republics and other ideal governments; which display, indeed, the wit, the humanity, and the goodness of their authors, but which never have had nor ever will have any influence on human affairs....

I know that those general principles which tend to enlighten and improve the human race are not absolutely useless ... that the enlightenment of nations is not without some effect on their rulers ... provided that the prerogative of the latter, their power, their security, their authority, their safety, is not touched thereby.... I know well that this general enlightenment, so much boasted of, is a beautiful and glorious chimera, with which philosophers love to amuse themselves, but which would soon disappear if they would open history, and see therefrom to what causes improved institutions are due. The nations of antiquity

8 The letter is in Diderot's *Œuvres*, ix. 451-66.

have passed, and those of the present will pass, before philosophy and its influence have reformed a single government....

... The cries of sages and philosophers are as the cries of the innocent man on the wheel, where they have never prevented, nor will ever prevent him from expiring, with his eyes upturned to heaven, which will perhaps some day stir up enthusiasm, or religious madness, or some other avenging folly, to accomplish all that their wisdom has failed to do. It is never the oration of the philosopher which disarms the powerful ruler; it is something else, which the combination of chance events brings about. Meanwhile we must not seek to force it from him, but must entreat humbly for such good as he can grant us, that is which he can grant us without injury to himself.

Ramsay was so far right, that whether a revolution was the only hope for theories like Beccaria's or not, the realisation of many of them was one of the first results of that general revolution, which seemed to Ramsay so impossible and undesirable. His letter, as it is a characteristic expression of that common apathy and despair of change which afflict at times even the most sanguine and hopeful, so it is, from its misplaced despair, a good cure for moods of like despondency. For the complete triumph of Beccaria's theories about torture, to say nothing of other improvements in law that he lived to witness, is perhaps the most signal instance in history of the conquest of theory over practice. For albeit that his theory was at total variance with the beliefs and ideas of the whole practical school, Beccaria lived to see torture abolished, not only in Lombardy and Tuscany, but in Austria generally, in Portugal and in Sweden, in Russia as well as in France. Yet Ramsay's fears at the time were more reasonable than the hopes of Beccaria.

There was little of eventfulness in Beccaria's life, and the only episode in it of interest was his visit to Paris in 1766. Thither he and his friend Pietro had been invited by Morellet, in the name of the philosophers at Paris, and thither he started in October 1766; not with Pietro, who could not leave Milan, but with Alessandro Verri, on a journey which was to include London as well as Paris, and was to occupy in all a period of six months.

A few years earlier Beccaria could have imagined no greater honour. To associate with the philosophers he so highly reverenced, as a philosopher himself, what greater happiness or reward could he have asked? Yet when it came there was no charm in it; and it was with difficulty he could be persuaded to go. For with his love for distinction there came into competition the love of his wife, and if he preferred her company to that of the wisest and wittiest celebrities of Paris, who shall say that he was the worse philosopher for that?

When the visit to Paris was contemplated it was a question of either not going at all or of leaving Teresa behind; there was not money enough for her to travel too. For Beccaria, though the son of a marquis and of noble origin, was not rich. When in his twenty-third year he married Teresa, his father was so opposed to the match on the score of insufficiency of fortune, that for some time after the marriage he refused to receive the young couple into his house, and they lived in considerable poverty. Appeal had even been made to the Government itself to break off, if possible, so unsuitable a match; but the lovers had their own way, of course, in the end, though it was not for some time that the domestic quarrel was healed, and then, it appears, through the mediation of Pietro Verri.

Beccaria would certainly have done better not to have gone to Paris at all. His letters to his wife during his absence show that he was miserable all the time. In every letter he calculates the duration of time that will elapse before his return, and there is an even current of distress and affection running through all the descriptions of his journey. The assurance is frequent that but for making himself ridiculous he would return at once. From Lyons he writes that he is in a state of the deepest melancholy; that even the French theatre he had so much looked forward to fails to divert him; and he begs his wife to prepare people for his speedy return by telling them that the air of France has a bad effect on his health.

Even when Paris was reached, and Beccaria and Alessandro were warmly welcomed by D'Alembert, Morellet, Diderot, and Baron Holbach, the homesickness remained. 'You would not believe,' says Beccaria to his wife, 'the welcomes, the politeness, the demonstrations of friendship and esteem, which they have shown to me and my companion. Diderot, Baron Holbach, and D'Alembert especially enchant us. The latter is a superior man, and most simple at the same time. Diderot displays enthusiasm and good humour in all he does. In short, nothing is wanting to me but yourself. All do their best to please me, and those who do so are the greatest men in Europe. All of them deign to listen to me, and no one shows the slightest air of superiority.' Yet Morellet tells us that even on arrival Beccaria was so absorbed in melancholy, that it was difficult to get four consecutive words from his mouth.

Six days after his arrival Beccaria writes in a similar strain: that he is in the midst of adorations and the most flattering praises, considered as the companion and colleague of the greatest men in Europe, regarded with admiration and curiosity, his company competed for; in the capital of pleasures, close to three theatres, one of them the Comédie Française, the most interesting spectacle in the world; and that yet he is unhappy and discontented, and unable to find distraction in anything. He tells his wife that he is in excellent health, but that she must say just the contrary, in order that there may be a good pretext for his return; and the better to ensure this, he sends his wife another letter which she may show to his parents, and in which, at the end of much general news about Paris, he alludes incidentally to the bad effect on his health of drinking the waters of the Seine. He regrets having to resort to this fiction; but considers that he is justified by the circumstances.

Accordingly he made a rapid journey back, leaving his companion to visit England alone; this expedition to Paris being the only event that ever broke the even tenor of his life. His French friends rather deserted him, Morellet in his memoirs going even so far as to speak of him as half-mad. But it was to his friendship with the Verris that this journey to Paris was most disastrous, and nothing is more mournful than the petty jealousies which henceforth completely estranged from him his early friends. The fault seems to have rested mainly with the two brothers, whose letters (only recently published) reveal an amount of bitterness against Beccaria for which it is difficult to find any justification, and which disposes for ever of all claims of their writers to any real nobleness of character.[9] They complain to one another of Beccaria's Parisian airs, of his literary pride, of his want of gratitude; they rejoice to think that his reputation is on the wane; that his illustrious friends at Paris send him no copies of their books; that he gets no letters from Paris; nay, they even go so far as to welcome the adverse criticisms of his 'Dei Delitti,' and to hope that his 'golden book' is shut up for ever.[10]-Alessandro writes to his brother that all his thoughts are turned to the means of mortifying Beccaria; and the revenge the brothers think most likely to humiliate him is for Alessandro to extend the limits of his travels, so as to compare favourably with Beccaria in the eyes of the Milanese. They delight in calling him a

9 See the two volumes of their *Lettere* published at Milan by Dr. C. Casati, 1880.

10 *Lettere*, ii. 221: 'Il suo libro d'oro sicuro è chiuso.'

madman, an imbecile, a harlequin; they lend a ready ear to all that gossip says in his discredit.[11] In the most trifling action Pietro sees an intended slight, and is especially sore where his literary ambition is touched.[12] It angers him that Beccaria should receive praise for the Apology written against Facchinei, the work having been entirely written by himself, with some help from his brother, but with not so much as a comma from the hand of Beccaria.[13] Some books which Beccaria had brought to him from Paris he imagined were really gifts to him from the authors; he believed that D'Alembert had sent him his 'Mélanges' of his own accord, not at the request of Beccaria, as the latter had represented; but even Alessandro admits that it was concerning the books, as Beccaria had said.[14] In short, the whole correspondence shows that Pietro Verri was extremely jealous of the success which he himself had helped his friend to attain, and that disappointed literary vanity was the real explanation of his suddenly transmuted affection.

But, to turn from this unpleasant episode of Beccaria's life, Catharine II., soon after his return to Milan, invited him to St. Petersburg, to assist in the preparation of her intended code of laws. It would seem from one of Pietro Verri's letters that Beccaria was at first inclined to accept the proposal,[15] but it is improbable that any such offer would really have tempted him to exchange Italian suns for Russian snows, even if Kaunitz and Firmian had not resolved to remove the temptation, by making his talents of service at home. This they did by making him Professor of Political Economy in the Palatine School of Milan, in November 1768; and his published lectures on this subject form the largest work he ever wrote.

There is no need to follow in further detail the life of Beccaria, for from this time to his death twenty-six years afterwards he never did nor wrote

---

11 *Lettere*, ii. 150.

12 Pietro had sent some of his manuscripts to Morellet, perhaps in the hope that the latter would offer to translate them. Anyhow Beccaria brought back no compliments to Pietro from Paris, and the key to Pietro's feelings lies in the words he wrote to his brother the day after Beccaria's return: 'Non mi ha detto una sillaba che mostri che alcuno sappia in Parigi, che io sono al mondo.'

13 *Lettere*, i. 391; ii. 70, 127, 151, 211, 295. It is satisfactory for this point to be settled, for even so lately as 1862, Sig. Cantù, in his work on Beccaria, attributes the *Risposta* to him, saying that all the intrinsic proofs are in favour of its being his work. P. 58.

14 *Ibid.* ii. 159.

15 *Lettere*, ii. 225.

anything which again placed him conspicuously in the world's eye.[16] His time was divided between the calls of his family and his country, but even as a member of the Government he never filled any very important post nor distinguished himself in any way above his colleagues. Three years before his death he became a member of a committee for the reform of the civil and criminal jurisprudence, and he and his former friend Pietro Verri lived to see many of the ideals of their youth become the actualities of their manhood, themselves helping to promote their accomplishment. It is characteristic of Beccaria that on two several occasions, when the King of Naples came to visit him in his house, he absented himself purposely from the irksomeness of an interview. So he lived to the age of fifty-six, little noticed by the world, a lover of solitude rather than of society, preferring a few friends to many acquaintances, leading a quiet and useful life, but to the last true to the philosophy he had professed in his youth, that it is better to live as a spectator of the world than as one with any direct interest in the game.

16 Morellet, Mémoires, i. 167: 'Revenu à Milan il a fait peu de chose, et sa fin n'a pas répondu à son début, phénomène commun parmi les gens de lettres d'Italie, qui ont un premier feu bien vif, mais qui, à 25 et 30 ans, se désabusent comme Salomon et reconnaissent que la science est vanité, sans avoir attendu d'être aussi savant que lui.'

CHAPTER II

The General Influence of Beccaria on Legislation

It is not easy in the days of a milder administration of penal laws than a century ago the most sanguine could have dreamed of to do full justice to those who laboured, as Beccaria and his friends did, at the peril of their lives and liberties, for those very immunities which we now enjoy. We cannot conceive that it should ever have been necessary to argue against torture, or that it should have been a bold thing to do so; still less can we conceive that it should ever have had its defenders, or that men should have been contented with the sophism, that it was indeed an evil, but an evil which was necessary and inevitable.

The very success of Beccaria's work has so accustomed us to its result that we are apt to regard it, as men regard a splendid cathedral in their native town, with very little recognition of its claims to admiration. The work is there, they see it, they live under its shadow; they are even ready to boast of it; but what to them is the toil and risk of its builders, or the care and thought of its architects? It may be said that this indifference is the very consummation Beccaria would most have desired, as it is the most signal proof of the success of his labour. So signal, indeed, has been that success, that already the atrocities which men in those days accepted as among the unalterable conditions of their existence, or resigned themselves to as the necessary safeguards of society, have become so repulsive to the world's memory, that men have agreed to hide them from their historical consciousness by seldom reading, writing, or speaking of their existence. And this is surely a fact to be remembered with hopefulness, when we hear an evil like war with all its attendant atrocities, defended nowadays by precisely the same arguments which little more than a hundred years ago were urged on behalf of torture, but which have proved nevertheless insufficient to keep it in existence.

It may be asked, How far was Beccaria the first to protest against the cruelty and absurdity of torture? To this it must be replied that although actually he was not the first, he was the first to do so with effect. The difference between previous writers on the subject and Beccaria is the difference between a man whose ideas are in advance of those of his age and a man who raises the ideas of his age to a level with his own. So early as the sixteenth century Montaigne, in his 'Essay on Conscience,' had said plainly enough that the putting a man to the rack was rather a trial of patience than of truth; that pain was as likely to extort a false confession as a true one; and that a judge, by having a man racked that he might not die innocent, caused him to die both innocent and racked. Also Grevius Clivensis wrote a work whilst in prison in Amsterdam, in which he sought to prove that torture was iniquitous, fallacious, and unchristian[17] This was published in 1624; and nearly a century later a Jesuit, Spee, wrote against the use of torture, as also against the cruel practices in force against witches.[18] And in later days Montesquieu, twenty years before Beccaria, had gone so far as to say that, since a civilised nation like England had abandoned torture without evil consequences, it was therefore unnecessary; but he followed the subject to no definite conclusion.

Beccaria himself was ready enough to refer all his thoughts to French inspiration, and to lay aside all claim to originality, with respect to which D'Alembert once wrote to him: 'A man such as you has no need of a master, still less of a master like myself. You are like the Titus Curtius of Tacitus, *ex se natus*, nor have your offspring any grandparent. A father like yourself is enough for them.'

But the honour of having been the first country to lay aside the use of torture undoubtedly belongs to England, just as the honour of having been the first in modern times to abolish capital punishment, except for political offences, belongs to Russia; and the practical example thus afforded by our laws probably did more for the general abolition of the custom than any written treatise on the subject ever would have done alone. English and foreign jurists long delighted to honour the Common Law for its non-recognition of torture. But though torture was contrary to the Common Law, and even to Magna Charta, it was not contrary to Prerogative; and until the Commonwealth it was used as matter of course in all grave accusations at the mere discretion of the monarch and Privy Council.[19] Therefore Beccaria pointed to England as a country which did not use torture with more justice than Grotius had done, who,

17 Cantù, Beccaria, 42.

18 In a book called *Cautio Criminalis*, published in 1718.

19 Jardine's *Reading on Torture.*

when the rack was still in use amongst us, quoted England as a proof that people might safely live without torture.

It is of interest to trace some of the practical results which followed Beccaria's treatise during the thirty years that he lived after its publication; that is, from the year 1764 to 1794.

The country in which the first attempt was made to apply his principles to practice was Russia, where Catharine II. was anxious to establish a uniform penal code, based on the liberal ideas of the time, which then found more favour in St. Petersburg than they did at Paris. For this purpose in 1767 she summoned to Moscow from all the provinces of Russia those 652 deputies who formed the nearest approach in the history of that country to a Russian Parliament. In the instructions that were read to this assembly, as the basis for the proposed codification of the laws, the principles propounded were couched not only in the spirit but often in the very words of the author of the 'Crimes and Punishments.' The following are examples:—

Laws should only be considered as a means of conducting mankind to the greatest happiness.

It is incomparably better to prevent crimes than to punish them.

The aim of punishment is not to torment sensitive beings.

All punishment is unjust that is unnecessary to the maintenance of public safety.

In methods of trial the use of torture is contrary to sound reason. Humanity cries out against the practice and insists on its abolition.

Judgment must be nothing but the precise text of the law, and the office of the judge is only to pronounce whether the action is contrary or conformable to it.

In the ordinary state of society the death of a citizen is neither useful nor necessary.

The following especially is from Beccaria:—

Would you prevent crimes, contrive that the laws favour less different orders of citizens than each citizen in particular. Let men fear the laws and nothing but the laws. Would you prevent crimes, provide that reason and knowledge be more and more diffused. To conclude: the surest but most difficult method of making men better is by perfecting education.[20]

Although these instructions were not so much laws as suggestions of laws, it is obvious what their effect must have been when published and diffused throughout Russia. That they were translated into Latin, German, French, and Italian proves the interest that was taken in Europe by this first attempt to apply the maxims of philosophy to practical government.

In France Beccaria's book became widely popular, and many writers helped to propagate his ideas, such as Servan, Brissot, Lacretelle, and Pastoret. Lacretelle attributes the whole impulse of criminal law reform to Beccaria, while regretting that Montesquieu had not said enough to attract general attention to the subject. His book is said to have so changed the spirit of the old French criminal tribunals, that, ten years before the Revolution, they bore no resemblance to their former selves. All the younger magistrates gave their judgments more according to the principles of Beccaria than according to the text of the law.[21] The result of the agitation appeared in the Royal Ordinances of 1780 and 1788, directed to the diminution of torture, the only reforms which preceded the Revolution. It is said that the last time anyone was tortured in France was in the year 1788, the last year of the *ancien régime*. At the very beginning of the Revolution more than a hundred different offences ceased to incur the penalty of death.

The most successful adoption of Beccaria's principles of punishment occurred in Tuscany, under the Grand Duke Leopold. When he ascended the ducal throne, the Tuscans were the most abandoned people of all Italy. Robberies and murders were none the less frequent for all the gallows, wheels, and tortures which were employed to repress them. But Leopold in 1786 resolved to try Beccaria's plan, for which purpose he published a code, proportioning punishments to crimes, abolishing mutilation and torture, reducing the number of acts of treason, lessening confiscations, destroying the right of asylum, and above all abolishing capital punishment even for murder. The result was, says a contemporary, that Tuscany, from having been the land of the greatest crimes and

20 Tooke's *Catharine II.*, 441-8. Rambaud's *Russie*, 476. 'Dans l'instruction pour la confection du nouveau Code, Catharine II., suivant sa propre expression, avait *pillé* les philosophes d'Occident, mais surtout Montesquieu et Beccaria.'

21 Morellet, *Mémoires*, i. 165.

villanies, became 'the best ordered State of Europe.'[22] During twenty years only five murders were committed in Tuscany, whilst at Rome, where death continued to be inflicted with great pomp, as many as sixty were committed within the space of three months.[23]

Torture was definitely and totally abolished in Portugal in 1776, in Sweden in 1786,[24] and in Austria in 1789. In the latter country, indeed, it had been abolished by Maria Theresa sixteen years before in her German and Polish provinces; and the Penal Code of Joseph II., published in 1785, was an additional tribute to the cause of reform. Secret orders were even given to the tribunals to substitute other punishments for hanging, yet so that the general public should be unaware of the change. There was the greatest anxiety that it should not be thought that this change was out of any deference for Beccaria or his school. 'In the abolition of capital punishment,' said Kaunitz, 'his Majesty pays no regard at all to the principles of modern philosophers, who, in affecting a horror of bloodshed, assert that primitive justice has no right to take from a man that life which Nature only can give him. Our sovereign has only consulted his own conviction, that the punishment he wishes substituted for the capital penalty is more likely to be felt by reason of its duration, and therefore better fitted to inspire malefactors with terror.'

Nor was it only in Europe that Beccaria's influence thus prevailed, for as soon as the American Colonies had shaken off their English connection they began to reform their penal laws. When the Revolution began there were in Pennsylvania nearly twenty crimes punishable by death, and within eighteen years of its close the penal code was thoroughly transformed, it being ordained in 1794 that no crime should any longer be capital but murder in the first degree. It is true that this was but a return to the principles adopted by Penn on the settlement of the colony, but Penn's penal code was annulled by Queen Anne, and the English Government insisted on a strict adherence to the charter from Charles II., which enjoined the retention of the Statute and the Common Law of England. When, therefore, the new Constitution was formed in 1776, the arguments of Beccaria gave fresh life to the memories of Penn.[25]

22 *General C. Lee's Memoirs.*

23 This fact rests on the authority of a gentleman of Pisa, who told it to Dr. Rush, the so-called 'American Æsculapius,' who wrote against capital punishment towards the end of the last century.

24 By Gustavus III. It had, however, been discontinued long before, as Beccaria speaks of it as non-existent when he wrote.

25 Turnbull's *Visit to Philadelphia Prison*, 1797.

Thus before his death Beccaria saw torture almost entirely abolished in Europe, and a general tendency spreading to follow the spirit of the changes he advocated in other details of criminal law. Probably no other theorist ever lived to witness so complete an adoption of his principles in practice, or so thorough a transformation of the system he attacked. It is possible that he but gave body and voice to ideas of change already widely prevalent in his time; but the merit of a man belongs none the less to himself, who changes the instability of public opinion into an active and solid force, and who gives distinct expression to the longings vaguely felt by a multitude.

But if the interest of Beccaria's chapter on Torture is now merely historical, an interest that is actual still attaches to his advocacy of the total abolition of capital punishment, this being the cause with which his name is most generally associated, and for which it is likely to be longest remembered. Previous writers, like Montaigne, if they deprecated the excess or severity of the death penalty, never thought of urging that it should be abolished altogether.

There is an apparent discrepancy in Beccaria's first condemning death as too severe a punishment and then recommending lifelong servitude as one of more deterrent power; but Beccaria would have said that the greater certainty of the latter more than compensated for the greater severity of the other. As regards the relative power of the two punishments, it probably varies in different individuals, some men having a greater dread of the one, and some of the other. The popular theory certainly goes too far, when it assumes that all men have a greater dread of the gallows than of anything else. When George III. once granted a pardon to the female convicts in Newgate on condition of their transportation to New South Wales, though seventeen of them accepted the offer, there were yet six who preferred death to a removal from their native country. It is also stated by Howard that in Denmark the punishment in cases of infanticide, namely, imprisonment for life, with labour and an annual whipping on the place of the crime, was 'dreaded more than death,' which it superseded as a punishment.

It is, however, probable that the frequency of any crime bears little or no relation to the punishment affixed to it. Every criminal begins a new career, in which he thinks less of the nature of his punishment than of his chances of eluding it. Neither tradition nor example count with him for much in his balance of the chances in his own favour. The law can never be so certain in its execution as it is uncertain in its application, and it is the examples of impunity, not of punishment, to which men turn when they violate the law. So that whether the punishment for murder be an excruciating death, as in ancient Rome, or a mere fine, as in ancient England, the motives for escape are always the same, the means to effect it are always the same, and the belief in his power to effect it is correspondingly powerful in every criminal guilty of homicide.

Even if we assume that death is absolutely the severest penalty devisable by the law, and that as a punishment for murder it is not too severe, it remains certain, that, relatively to the circumstances of a trial for murder, to the reluctance of judges or juries to pass an irretrievable sentence, to their fear of error, to their conscientious regard for human life, it is really a much less terrible danger for a malefactor to face than a penalty which would justify fewer hopes of impunity.

Nor are such scruples to convict unreasonable, when we consider the number who on apparently conclusive evidence have been falsely and irrevocably condemned to death. Playgoers who have seen 'The Lyons Mail' will remember how barely Lesurques, the Parisian gentleman, escaped punishment for the guilt of Dubosc, the robber and murderer. But the moral of the story is lost in the play, for Lesurques actually was executed for the crime of Dubosc, by reason of the strong resemblance he bore to him, the latter only receiving the due reward for his crimes after the innocent man had died as a common murderer on the scaffold. Then there are cases in which, as in the famous case of Calas, some one having committed suicide, some one else is executed as the murderer. That dead men tell no tales is as true of men hung as of men murdered, and the innocence of an executed man may be proved long afterwards or not at all.

Where there is no capital punishment, as in Michigan, a man's innocence may be discovered subsequently to conviction, and justice done to him for the error of the law. Such a case actually happened not long ago in Michigan, where a prisoner's innocence was clearly proved after ten years' imprisonment. Where capital punishment exists, there is no such hope; nor is there any remedy if, as in the case of Lewis, who was hung in 1831, another man thirty-three years afterwards confesses himself the murderer. It is impossible to preclude all chances of such errors of justice. Illustrative of this is the story of the church organist near Kieff, who murdered a farmer with a pistol he stole from a priest.

After his crime he placed the pistol in the sacristy, and then, when he had prevented the priest from giving evidence against him by the act of confession, went and denounced the priest as the culprit. The priest, in spite of his protestations of innocence, was sentenced to hard labour for life; and when, twenty years afterwards, the organist confessed his guilt on his deathbed, and the priest's liberation was applied for, it was found that he had died only a few months before.[26]

That the scruple to convict diminishes the certainty of punishment, and therefore raises hopes of impunity, is illustrated by the case of two American brothers who, desirous to perpetrate a murder, waited till their victim had left their State, in which capital punishment had been abolished, and had betaken himself to a State which still retained it, before they ventured to execute their criminal intention. That such reluctance to convict is often most injurious to the public is proved by the case of a woman at Chelmsford who some years ago was acquitted, in spite of strong evidence, on a charge of poisoning, and who, before her guilt was finally proved, lived to poison several other persons who would otherwise have escaped her arts.[27]

Such considerations as these will, perhaps, lead some day to the abolition of capital punishment. The final test of all punishment is its efficiency, not its humanity. There is often more inhumanity in a long sentence of penal servitude than in a capital sentence, for the majority of murderers deserve as little mercy as they get. The many offences which have ceased to be capital in English law yielded less to a sense of the inhumanity of the punishment as related to the crime than to the experience that such a punishment led to almost total impunity. The bankers, for instance, who petitioned Parliament to abolish capital punishment for forgery, did so, as they said, because they found by experience that the infliction of death, or the possibility of its infliction, prevented the prosecution, the conviction, and the punishment of the criminal; therefore they begged for 'that protection for their property which they would derive from a more lenient law.'

For the same reason it is of little avail to call in question, as Beccaria does, the right of society to inflict death as a punishment. There may be a distinction between the right of society and its might, but it is one of little

26 *Times*, March 1, 1880.

27 For most of the above facts the writer is indebted to the papers published by the Howard Association, kindly sent to him by the Secretary, Mr. Tallack.

comfort to the man who incurs its resentment. A man in a dungeon does better to amuse himself with spiders and cobwebs than with reflections on the encroachment of the law upon his liberty, or with theories about the rights of government. Whenever society has ceased to exercise any of its powers against individuals, it has not been from the acceptance of any new doctrine as to its rights, but from more enlightened views as to its real interests, and a cultivated dislike of cruelty and oppression.

When Beccaria wrote against capital punishment, one great argument against its abolition was its practical universality. It had been abolished in ancient Egypt by king Sabaco,[28] in the best period of the Roman Republics by the Porcian law, and in the time of the Roman Empire by Calo-Johannes.[29] But these cases were too remote from modern times to lend much weight to the general argument. At that time Russia alone of all the countries in the world had, from the accession of the Empress Elizabeth, afforded a practical example of the fact, that the general security of life is not diminished by the withdrawal of the protection of capital punishment. But since that time this truth has become less and less a theory or speculation, and it now rests on the positive experience of no inconsiderable portion of the world. In Tuscany, Holland, Portugal, Russia, Roumania, Saxony, Prussia, Belgium, and in ten of the United States of America, the death penalty has either been abolished or discontinued; and can it be thought that the people of those countries are so indifferent to the safety of their lives as to be content with a less efficient legal protection than is vouchsafed in countries where the protection is death?

The opponents of capital punishment may fairly, therefore, draw an argument in their favour from the fact that so many parts of the world have found it not incompatible with the general security of life to erase the death penalty from their list of deterrent agencies. It is better to rely on so plain a fact than on statistics which, like two-edged weapons, often cut both ways. The frequency of executions in one country and their total absence in another may severally coexist with great numerical equality in the number of murders committed in each. It is always better, therefore, to look for some other cause for a given number of murders than the kind of punishment directed to their repression. They may depend on

---

28 Diodorus Siculus, i. 65: ντ γρ το θαν του το ς καταδικασθ ντας ν γκαζε λειτουργε ν τα ς π λεσι δεδεμ νους.

29 Gibbon, c. 48: 'During his government of twenty-five years the penalty of death was abolished in the Roman Empire.' A.D. 1118-1143.

a thousand other things, which it is difficult to ascertain or eliminate. Thus both in Bavaria, where capital punishment has been retained, and in Switzerland, where it had been abolished in 1874, murders have increased greatly in recent years; and this fact has, with great probability, been attributed to the influence of bad habits contracted during the Franco-German war.

Capital punishment being less general in the world now than torture was when Beccaria wrote, it seems to be a fair logical inference that it is already far advanced towards its total disappearance. For the same argument which Voltaire applied in the case of torture cannot fail sooner or later to be applied to capital punishment. 'If,' he says, 'there were but one nation in the world which had abolished the use of torture; and if in that nation crimes were no more frequent than in others, ... its example would be surely sufficient for the rest of the world. England alone might instruct all other nations in this particular; but England is not the only nation. Torture has been abolished in other countries, and with success; the question, therefore, is decided.' If in this argument we read capital punishment instead of torture, murders instead of crimes, and Portugal instead of England, we shall best appreciate that which is after all the strongest argument against capital punishment, namely, that it has been proved unnecessary for its professed object in so many countries that it might safely be relinquished in all.

CHAPTER III

The Influence of Beccaria in England

Whatever improvement our penal laws have undergone in the last hundred years is due primarily to Beccaria, and to an extent that has not always been recognised. Lord Mansfield is said never to have mentioned his name without a sign of respect. Romilly referred to him in the very first speech he delivered in the House of Commons on the subject of law reform. And there is no English writer of that day who, in treating of the criminal law, does not refer to Beccaria.

Even the idea of public utility as the final test and standard of morality is derived from Beccaria, and the famous expression, 'the greatest happiness of the greatest number,' occurs, in capital letters, in the very first page of the 'Delitti e delle Pene.'[30] Bentham himself fully acknowledged this. 'Priestley was the first,' he says, 'unless it was Beccaria, who taught my lips to pronounce this sacred truth: that the greatest happiness of the greatest number is the foundation of morals and happiness.' And with reference to his idea of the measurable value of different pains and pleasures, he says: 'It was from Beccaria's little treatise on Crimes and Punishments that I drew, as I well remember, the first hint of this principle, by which the precision and clearness and incontestableness of mathematical calculations are introduced for the first time into the field of morals.'

English philosophy and legislation, therefore, owe enough to Beccaria for his treatise never to be forgotten among us. Standing, as it does, in reference to law as Bacon's 'Novum Organon' to science, or Descartes' 'Principia' to philosophy, and representing a return to first principles and rejection of mere precedent in the matter of penal laws, it will never fail to gratify those who, with little admiration for law in the concrete, can yet find pleasure in studying it in the abstract. Most men will turn readily from a system built up, as our own is, of unintelligible distinctions, and based on authority rather than on experience, to a system where no

30 Beccaria doubtless got the expression from Helvetius, who used it in his *L'Esprit*, i. 228, 291.

distinctions exist save those which are derived from the nature of things and are founded on the real differences that distinguish the moral actions of mankind.

The first trace of Beccaria's influence in England appeared in the first edition of Blackstone's Commentaries, of which the book on the Criminal Laws was published the very next year after the appearance of the Italian treatise. That Blackstone was well acquainted with it is proved by his frequent reference to it in treating of crimes. From Beccaria he argues that the certainty of punishments is more effectual than their severity, and finds it absurd to apply the same punishment to crimes of different malignity. Blackstone was also the first professional lawyer to find fault with the frequency of capital punishment in England, and to point out as 'a melancholy truth' the presence of 160 actions in the statute book which were felonies without benefit of clergy.

But there was one great fallacy, pervading our whole criminal law, which Blackstone left undetected and untouched. This was, that the severity of punishment must be augmented in proportion to the increase of temptation, and that the measure of the guilt of a crime lay in the facility with which it might be committed. 'Among crimes of an equal malignity,' says Blackstone, 'those [deserve most punishment, as most injurious] which a man has the most frequent and easy opportunities of committing, which cannot so easily be guarded against as others, and which, therefore, the offender has the strongest inducement to commit.' And on this principle he finds it reasonable, that, while the theft of a pocket-handkerchief should be a capital crime, the theft of a load of hay should only involve transportation.

There was not an anomaly in our old criminal practice which was not based on this theory—a theory which had, indeed, its precedent in the old Hebrew law that punished more severely a theft from a field than a theft from a house; and the first writer who protested against it was Eden, afterwards Lord Auckland, who in 1771 published his 'Principles of Penal Law,' one of the best books ever written on the subject. The influence of Beccaria is apparent in Eden's work, not only by his direct reference to it, but by his spirit of declared opposition to the actual practice of the law. Two instances of its tendency will suffice. 'Imprisonment, inflicted by law as a punishment, is not according to the principles of wise legislation. It sinks useful subjects into burthens on the community, and has always a bad effect on their morals; nor can it communicate the benefit of example, being in its nature secluded from the eye of the people.' And again: 'Whatever exceeds simple death is mere cruelty. Every step beyond is a trace of ancient barbarity, tending only to distract the attention of the spectators and to lessen the solemnity of the example. There is no such thing as vindictive justice; the idea is shocking.'

Men of letters as a rule did not speak with this boldness, but in conscious opposition to professional and popular feeling expressed their doubts with a hesitation that was almost apologetic. So, for example, Goldsmith could not 'avoid even questioning the validity of that right which social combinations have assumed of capitally punishing offences of a slight nature.'[31] Strange, that in England such an argument should ever have seemed a daring novelty, a thing to be said tentatively and with reserve!

Lord Kames attacked our criminal law in a still more indirect way, by tracing punishment historically to the revenge of individuals for their private injuries, and by extolling the excellence of the criminal law of the ancient Egyptians. They, he said, avoided capital punishments as much as possible, preferring others which equally prevented the recommission of crimes. Such punishments effected their end 'with less harshness and severity than is found in the laws of any other nation, ancient or modern.'[32]

Nothing could be more interesting than Lord Kames' account of the growth of criminal law, from the rude revenges of savages to the legal punishments of civilised States; but it was probably intended by its author less as an historical treatise than as a veiled attack upon the penal system of his country. It is, therefore, a good illustration of the timidity of the Theoretical school against the overwhelming forces of the Practical school of law, which, of course, included the great body of the legal profession; and it is the first sign of an attempt to apply the experience of other countries and times to the improvement of our own jurisprudence.

It certainly should moderate our reverence for ancestral wisdom to find even a man like Fielding, the novelist, speaking, in his Charge to the Grand Jury of Middlesex, of the pillory and the loss of a man's ears as

31 *Vicar of Wakefield*, c. 27; and *Citizen of the World*, letter 79. Johnson was more outspoken in the *Rambler*, No. 114 (1751), in which he advocated the restriction of capital punishment to cases of murder.

32 Lord Kames' *Historical Law Tracts. Criminal Law.* 1776.

'an extremely mild' punishment for a bad case of libel, or declaring our punishments of that time to be 'the mildest and most void of terror of any other in the known world.' Yet Fielding recognised several of the true principles of punishment. He attributed the increase of crime to the great abuse of pardons, which, he said, had brought many more men to the gallows than they had saved from it. He also advocated the diminution of the number of executions, their greater privacy and solemnity, whilst he recommended their following as closely as possible on conviction, that pity for the criminal might be lost in detestation for his crime.[33]

But that the humanity of the speculative school of law was not without some influence on public opinion, as well as to a certain extent a reflection of it, is proved by a few abortive attempts in Parliament to mitigate the severity of our penal code in the latter half of the last century. Even so early as 1752 the Commons agreed to commute the punishment of felony in certain cases to hard labour in the docks; but the Lords refused their consent, as from that time onward for more than eighty years they regularly continued to refuse it to all mitigation of the laws affecting crime. It must ever remain a matter of regret, that the *rôle* of the House of Lords in the matter of criminal law reform should have continued from 1752 to 1832 to be one of systematic and obstinate opposition to change, and an opposition which had no justification in the general level of national enlightenment.

The chief honour of the earliest attempt at law reform belongs to Sir William Meredith, who in 1770 moved for a committee of inquiry into the state of the criminal laws. This committee proposed in its report of the following year the repeal of a few Acts which made certain offences capital; and accordingly the Commons in 1772 agreed, that it should no longer be punishable as high treason to make an attempt on the life of a Privy Councillor, that desertion of officers or soldiers should no longer be capital, nor the belonging to people who called themselves Egyptians. Some other proposals were negatived, such as a repeal of the hard law of James I. against infanticide; but the House of Lords refused their assent even to the slight changes passed by the Commons. 'It was an innovation, they said, and subversion of the law.'[34] It is no reproach to Meredith, Burke, and Fox that they ceased to waste their strength against Conservatism such as this. All hope of reform was out of the question; and the most dreadful atrocities were suffered or defended. In 1777 a girl

33 *Enquiry into the Late Increase of Robbers* (1751).

34 Meredith's speech of May 13, 1777, in *Parl. Deb.*, xix. 239.

of 14 lay in Newgate under sentence to be burnt alive for false coinage, because some whitewashed farthings, that were to pass for sixpences, were found on her person; and a reprieve only came just as the cart was ready to take her to the stake. Not till 1790 was the law abolished by which women were liable to be burnt publicly for high or petit treason.[35]

But whatever tendency might have been arising in theory or in practice about this time to mitigate the severity of our laws was destined to receive a dead check from the publication in 1784 and 1785 respectively of two books which deserve historical recollection. The first was Madan's 'Thoughts on Executive Justice,' in which the author, adopting Beccaria's principle of the certainty of punishment as the best check on crime, advocated an unflinching carrying out of the laws as they stood. 'It was,' says Romilly, 'a strong and vehement censure upon the judges and the ministers for their mode of administering the law, and for the frequency of the pardons which they granted. It was very much read, and certainly was followed by the sacrifice of many lives.'

The year before its publication 51 malefactors were executed in London, the year after 97, whilst not long afterwards was seen the rare spectacle of nearly 20 criminals hung at a time. Romilly was so much shocked at what he considered the folly and inhumanity of Madan's book that he wrote a short tract of observations upon it, of which he sent a copy to each of the judges. But it is characteristic of the feeling of that time that only a hundred copies of his tract were sold. It was, however, from that time that Romilly began to make the criminal law his special study, so that to Madan indirectly our country owes the efforts of Romilly.

The other book was from a man whom above all others our forefathers delighted to honour. This was Archdeacon Paley, who in 1785 published his 'Moral and Political Philosophy,' and dedicated it to the then Bishop of Carlisle. Nor is this fact of the dedication immaterial, for the said Bishop was the father of the future Lord Chief Justice Ellenborough, who enjoys the melancholy fame of having been the inveterate and successful opponent of nearly every movement made in his time, in favour of the mitigation of our penal laws. The chapter on Crimes and Punishments in Paley and the speeches of Lord Ellenborough on the subject in the House of Lords are, in point of fact, the same thing; so that Paley's chapter is of distinct historical importance, as the chief cause of the obstruction of reform, and as the best expression of the philosophy of his day. If

35 Lecky's *England*, i. 506.

other countries adopted Beccaria's principles more quickly than our own, it was simply that those principles found no opponents anywhere equal to Archdeacon Paley and his pupil, Lord Ellenborough.

Paley, of course, defended the thing he found established; nor, considering the system he had to defend, did he state the case for it without ingenuity. He had, indeed, nothing to add to what Blackstone had said regarding punishment, namely, that it was inflicted, not in proportion to the real guilt of an offence, but in proportion to its facility of commission and difficulty of detection. To steal from a shop was not more criminal than to steal from a house, but, as it was more difficult to detect, it was more severely punished. Sheep, horses, and cloth on bleaching-grounds were more exposed to thieves than other kinds of property; therefore their theft required a stronger deterrent penalty.

There was only one offence which Paley thought the English law punished too severely, and that was the offence of privately stealing from the person. In all other cases he defended the application of the capital penalty. It was, he thought, the peculiar merit of the English law that it swept into the net every crime which under any possible circumstance might merit death, whilst it only singled out a few cases in each class of crime for actual punishment; so that whilst few really suffered death, the dread and danger of it hung over the crimes of many. The law was not cruel, for it was never meant to be indiscriminately executed, but left a large margin for the exercise of mercy.

Paley agreed with Beccaria that the certainty of punishment was of more consequence than its severity. For this reason he recommended 'undeviating impartiality in carrying the laws into execution;' he blamed the 'weak timidity' of juries, leading them to be over-scrupulous about the certainty of their evidence, and protested against the maxim that it was better for ten guilty men to escape than for one innocent man to perish. A man who fell by a mistaken sentence might, he argued, be considered as falling for his country, because he was the victim of a system of laws which maintained the safety of the community.

Such was the reasoning which for nearly half a century governed the course of English history, and which for all that time it was a heresy to dispute.

Barbarous spectacles were, Paley thought, justly found fault with, as tending to demoralise public feeling. 'But,' he continued, 'if a mode of execution could be devised which would augment the horror of the punishment, without offending or impairing the public sensibility by cruel or unseemly exhibitions of death, it might add something to the efficacy of example; and by being reserved for a few atrocious crimes might also enlarge the scale of punishment, an addition to which seems wanting, for as the matter remains at present you hang a malefactor for a simple robbery, and can do no more to the villain who has poisoned his father. Something of the sort we have been describing was the proposal, not long since suggested, of casting murderers into a den of wild beasts, where they would perish in a manner dreadful to the imagination, yet concealed from the view.' It is interesting after this to learn, that Paley thought torture properly exploded from 'the mild and cautious system of penal jurisprudence established in this country,' and that (to do him justice) he urged private persons to be tender in prosecuting, out of regard for the difficulty of prisoners to obtain an honest means of livelihood after their discharge.

Howard's book on the Lazarettos of Europe appeared four years after Paley's work. Although it did not deal directly with crimes, it indirectly treated of their connection with punishment. Howard was able to show that whilst in Middlesex alone 467 persons had been executed in nine years, only six had been executed in Amsterdam; that for a hundred years the average number of executions had been one a year at Utrecht and that for twenty-four years there had not even been one there. The inference therefore was that the diminution of punishment had a direct effect in diminishing crime. Howard also advocated the restriction of capital punishment to cases of murder, arson, and burglary; highwaymen, footpads, and habitual thieves should, he thought, end their days in a penitentiary rather than on the gallows. Even this was a bold proposal, in a state of society yet in bondage to Paley.

Something, however, occurred more fatal to the reform of our penal laws than even the philosophy of Paley, and that was the French Revolution. Before 1790 there had been 115 capital offences in France; so that to alter the criminal law in England was to follow a precedent of unpleasant auspices. Reform not unnaturally savoured of revolution, and especially a reform of the penal laws. In 1808 Romilly said he would advise anyone, who desired to realise the mischievous effects of the French Revolution in England to attempt some legislative reform on humane and liberal principles. With bitterness he tells the story of a young nobleman, who, addressing him insolently at the bar of the House of Commons, informed him that he for his part was for hanging all criminals. Romilly observed that he supposed he meant punishments should be certain and the laws executed, whatever they were. 'No, no,' was the reply, 'it isn't that. There is no good done by mercy. They only get worse: I would hang them all up at once.' And this represented the prevalent opinion. Windham, in a speech against the Shoplifting Bill, inquired, 'Had not the French Revolution begun with the abolition of capital punishment in every case?... Was such a system as this was to be set up without consideration against that of Dr. Paley!'[36]

Romilly's first idea with respect to the reform of the criminal law was a sufficiently humble one. It was nothing more than to raise the amount of the value of the property, the theft of which should expose a man to death. Twelvepence, as fixed by the statute of Elizabeth, originally signified a much greater theft than it had come to signify after a lapse of two centuries. Romilly had at first no idea of removing the death penalty for theft; his only hope was to get it affixed to a graver theft than the larceny of a shilling. Yet even so he could not bring himself to consult with the judges on the subject of his intended bill, for 'he had not the least hope they would approve of the measure.'

It was by the advice of Scarlett, Lord Abinger, that he ventured to aim at the repeal of all statutes punishing mere theft with death; but, deeming it hopeless to urge their abolition all at once, he resolved to begin with that famous statute of Elizabeth which made it a capital crime to steal a handkerchief or anything else from the person of another which was of the value of a shilling. His bill to effect this passed both Houses the same year it was introduced (1808), in spite of the strong opposition of the great legal dignitaries in either House. The statute was based, said Judge Burton, on the experience of two and a half centuries. The alternative punishment of transportation for seven years, said the Attorney-General, would be too short; it should be for more years than seven, if not for life. If any change of punishment were necessary, said Lord Ellenborough, it should be transportation for life.

Such was legal opinion generally as expressed by its ablest representatives with respect to the due punishment for pocket-picking not a hundred years ago. It is easy now to smile at such errors, and, at the barren waste of wisdom spent in their defence, but what weight after that can be attached, on subjects of the general policy of the law, to the

---

36 Speech, May 11, 1810.

opinion of its chief professors? Can it be too much regretted that Lord Chief Justice Ellenborough should have sacrificed to his own authority, whilst alive, the authority of all judges ever destined to succeed him?

The success which attended Romilly's Privately Stealing Bill and the failure which attended almost all his other efforts was probably due to the fact that larceny from the person without violence was, as has been said, the one single kind of offence which had Paley's sanction for ceasing to be capital. But the very success of his first bill was the chief cause of the failure of his subsequent ones. For, capital punishment having been removed for mere pilfering, prosecutions became more frequent, and the opponents of reform were thus able to declare that an increase of theft had been the direct consequence of the abolition of the capital penalty. It was in vain to point out, that the apparent increase of theft was due to the greater readiness of individuals to prosecute and of juries to convict, when a verdict of guilt no longer involved death as the consequence.

Romilly also injured his cause by a pamphlet on the criminal law, in which he criticised severely the doctrines of Paley. So strongly was this resented, that in 1810 his bill to abolish capital punishment for stealing forty shillings from a dwelling-house did not even pass the Commons, being generally opposed, as it was by Windham, because the maintenance of Paley's reputation was regarded as a great object of national concern.[37] That is to say, men voted not so much against the bill as against the author of a heresy against Paley.

In those days to steal five shillings' worth of goods from a shop was a capital offence, and Paley had explained the philosophy of the punishment. It would be tedious to follow the course of Romilly's bill against this law, called the Shoplifting Act, through the details of its history. Suffice it to say that it passed the Commons in 1810, 1811, 1813, 1816, but was regularly thrown out by the Lords, and only definitely became law many years later. But though the debates on the subject no longer possess the vivid interest that once belonged to them, and are best left to the oblivion that enshrouds them, it is instructive to take just one sample of the eloquence and arguments, that once led Lords and Bishops captive and expressed the highest legal wisdom obtainable in England.

Lord Ellenborough, on the last day but one of May 1810, appealed to their lordships to pause, before they passed the Shoplifting Bill and

37 Romilly's *Memoirs*, ii. 322.

gave their assent to the repeal of a law which had so long been held necessary for the security of the public. No one, he insisted, was more disposed than himself to the exercise of clemency, but there was not the slightest ground for the insinuations of cruelty that had been cast on the administration of the law. If shoplifting did not require the penalty of death, the same rule would have to apply to horse- and sheep-stealing; and, in spite of all that was said in favour of this speculative humanity, they must all agree, that prevention of crime should be the chief object of the law, and that terror alone could prevent the crime in question. Those who were thus speculating in modern legislation urged that punishment should be certain and proportionate; but he could satisfy the House that any attempt to apply a punishment in exact conformity to the offence would be perfectly ludicrous. He had consulted with the other judges, and they were *unanimously of opinion* that it would not be expedient to remit this part of the severity of the criminal law.[38]- He therefore entreated them to pause.

Need it be said that the House of Lords paused, as they were entreated to do, and that they paused and paused again, in a manner more suggestive of the full stop than the comma, generally out of deference to the same authority? Romilly was indignant that so many prelates voted against his bills; but could they have done otherwise, when the best legal authorities in England urged that it would be fatal to vote for them?—when they were gravely told that if a certain bill passed, they would not know whether they stood on their heads or on their feet?

Lord Ellenborough was so hard upon 'speculative humanity,' as opposed to real practical common sense, that the speculative school are never likely to forget him. But they owe too much to him not to forgive him; since he is the standing proof, that in matters of the general policy of the law professional opinion is a less trustworthy guide than popular sentiment, and that in questions of law reform it is best to neglect the fossil-wisdom of forgotten judges, and to seek the opinion of Jones round the corner as readily as that of Jones upon the Bench.

A strong feeling against the pillory was aroused by the sentence passed against Lord Cochrane in 1814, by which, for supposed complicity in a plot to raise the price of the Funds, he was condemned to a year's imprisonment, to a fine of 1000*l*., and to stand in the pillory. A bill for

38 Hansard, and Campbell's *Chief Justices*, iii. 233. The arguments are almost Paley's word for word.

the abolition of the pillory accordingly passed the Commons the very next year, but Lord Ellenborough succeeded again in bringing the Upper House to a pause: the pillory forsooth was as old as 1269; it was spoken of by the old historians; it was not confined to this country, for Du Cange spoke of it on the Continent. For these reasons the pillory remained a legal punishment down to the first year of the present reign.

Yet Lord Ellenborough was one of the best judges known to English history; he was, according to his biographer, a man 'of gigantic intellect,' and one of the best classical scholars of his day; and if he erred, it was with all honesty and goodness of purpose. The same must be said of Lord Chief Justice Tenterden's opposition to any change in the law of forgery. His great merits too as a judge are matter of history, yet when the Commons had passed the bill for the abolition of capital punishment for forgery, Lord Tenterden assured the House of Lords that they could not 'without great danger take away the punishment of death.' 'When it was recollected how many thousand pounds, and even tens of thousands, might be abstracted from a man by a deep-laid scheme of forgery, he thought that this crime ought to be visited with the utmost extent of punishment which the law then wisely allowed.' The House of Lords again paused in submission to judicial authority.

Sir James Mackintosh, who succeeded Romilly as law reformer, in 1820 introduced with success six penal reform bills into the House of Commons; but the Lords assented to none of them that were of any practical importance to the country. They agreed, indeed, that it should no longer be a capital offence for an Egyptian to reside one year in the country, or for a man to be found disguised in the Mint, or to injure Westminster Bridge; but they did not agree to remove the capital penalty for such offences as wounding cattle, destroying trees, breaking down the banks of rivers, or sending threatening letters. It was feared that if the punishment were mitigated, the whole of Lincolnshire might be submerged, whole forests cut down, and whole herds destroyed. As to the Shoplifting Bill, they would not let death be abolished for stealing in shops altogether, but only where the value of the theft was under 10*l*. That seemed the limit of safe concession.

Sir Robert Peel, who was the first Ministerial law reformer, succeeded in getting the death penalty repealed for several crimes which were practically obsolete, but forty kinds of forgery alone still remained capital offences.

So great, however, did the changes appear to be, that Sir James Mackintosh declared, towards the close of his life, that it was as if he had lived in two different countries, such was the contrast between the past and the present. Yet Sir James died in the very year that the first Reform Bill passed, and it was not till after that event that any really great progress was made towards ameliorating the penal laws.

It is well known that Lord Tenterden refused ever to sit again in the House of Lords if the Reform Bill became law, and that he predicted that that measure would amount to the political extinction of the Upper House. As regards the history of our criminal law Lord Tenterden was right, for the period of long pauses had passed away, and rapid changes were made with but short intervals of breathing-time. From the year the Reform Bill passed the school of Beccaria and Bentham achieved rapid successes in England. In 1832 it ceased to be capital to steal a horse or a sheep, in 1833 to break into a house, in 1834 to return prematurely from transportation, in 1835 to commit sacrilege or to steal a letter. But even till 1837 there were still 37 capital offences on the statute-book; and now there are only two, murder and treason. Hanging in chains was abolished in 1834; the pillory was wholly abolished in 1837; and the same year Ewart, after many years' struggle, obtained for prisoners on trial for felony the right (still merely a nominal one)[39] of being defended by counsel.

Thus it has come about that, after steady opposition and fierce conflict, English law finds itself at the very point which Johnson and Goldsmith had attained a hundred years before; so true is it, as Beccaria has said, that the enlightenment of a nation is always a century in advance of its practice. The victory has conclusively been with the ultra-philosophers, as they were once called, with the speculative humanitarians, for whom good Lord Ellenborough had so honest a contempt. Paley's philosophy has long since been forgotten, and if it affords any lesson at all, it lies chiefly in a comparison between his gloomy predictions and the actual results of the changes he deprecated. The practical and professional school of law has yielded on all the most important points to the dissolving influence of Beccaria's treatise; and the growing demand for increasing the security of human life by the institution of a penalty, more effective because more certain, than that at present in force, points to the still further triumph of Beccaria's principles, likely before long to mark the progress of his influence in England.

39 Stephen's *English Criminal Law*, 156, 178.

CHAPTER IV

The Problems of Penology

If we would bring to the study of Beccaria's treatise the same disposition of mind with which he wrote it, we must enter upon the subject with the freest possible spirit of inquiry, and with a spirit of doubtfulness, undeterred in its research by authority however venerable, by custom however extended, or by time however long. It has been from too great reverence for the wisdom of antiquity that men in all ages have consigned their lives and properties to the limited learning and slight experience of generations which only lived for themselves and had no thought of binding posterity in the rules they thought suitable to their own times. Beccaria sounded the first note of that appeal from custom to reason in the dominion of law which has been, perhaps, the brightest feature in the history of modern times, and is still transforming the institutions of all countries.

The object, therefore, of this chapter is chiefly negative, being none other than to raise such mistrust of mere custom, and so strong a sense of doubt, by the contradictions apparent in existing laws and theories, that the difficulties of their solution may tempt to some investigation of the principles on which they rest.

That Penology is still only in its experimental stage as a science, in spite of the progress it has made in recent times, is clear from the changes that are so constantly being made in every department of our penal system. We no longer mutilate nor kill our criminals, as our ancestors did in the plenitude of their wisdom; we have ceased to transport them, and our only study now is to teach them useful trades and laborious industry. Yet whether we shall better bring them to love labour by compulsory idleness or by compulsory work, whether short imprisonment or long is the most effective discipline, whether seclusion or association is least likely to demoralise them, these and similar questions have their answers in a quicksand of uncertainty. This only may experience be said to have yet definitely proved, that very little relation exists in any country between the given quantity of crime and the quantity or severity of punishment directed to its prevention. It has taken thousands of years to establish this truth, and even yet it is but partially recognised over the world.

It would appear at first sight that there could be little to say about crimes and punishments, so obvious and self-evident seem the relations that exist between them. Many people still believe in an innate sense of justice in mankind, sufficient always to prevent wide aberrations from equity. Is it, they might ask, conceivable that men should ever lose sight of the distinction between the punishment of guilt and the punishment of innocence?—that they should ever punish one equally with the other? Yet there is no country in the world which in its past or present history has not involved the relations of a criminal in the punishment inflicted on him; and in savage countries generally it is still common to satisfy justice with vengeance on some blood-relation of a malefactor who escapes from the punishment due to his crime.

It would also seem to demand no great insight to perceive that a voluntary intention must be a universal attribute of a criminal action. No one would think of punishing a man who in his sleep killed another, although, if the injury to society be the measure of punishment, his crime is equivalent to intentional homicide. Yet at Athens an involuntary murderer was banished until he could, give satisfaction to the relatives of the deceased; and in China, though the penal code generally separates intentional from accidental crimes, anyone who kills a near relation by accident or commits certain kinds of arson by accident undergoes different degrees of banishment and a fixed number of bamboo strokes.[40]

Even inanimate objects or animals it has been thought through many ages reasonable to punish. In Athens an axe or stone that killed anyone by accident was cast beyond the border; and the English law was only repealed in the present reign which made a cartwheel, a tree, or a beast, that killed a man, forfeit to the State for the benefit of the poor. The Jewish law condemned an ox that gored anyone to death to be stoned, just as it condemned the human murderer. And in the middle ages pigs, horses, or oxen were not only tried judicially like men, with counsel on either side and witnesses, but they were hung on gallows like men, for the better deterrence of their kind in future.[41]

---

40 Sir G. Staunton's *Penal Code of China*, 347, 416.

41 See several instances in Baring Gould's *Curiosities of Olden Times*, in the chapter on Queer Culprits.

These customs had doubtless their defenders, and left the world not without a struggle. It must have cost some one, whosoever first questioned the wisdom of hanging animals or murdering a criminal's relations, as much ridicule as it cost Beccaria to question the efficacy of torture or the right of capital punishment. But the boldness of thought in that unknown reformer was probably lost sight of in the arrogance of his profanity, and he doubtless paid with his own neck for his folly in defending the pig's.

It may be said that all such absurdities are past; that the Jews, the Athenians, the Chinese, the Europeans of the middle ages can scarcely be cited as reasonable beings; that they had no rational theory of punishment, and that their errors have been long since discarded. But at least their example suggests that even in our own system there may be inconsistencies and blemishes which custom and authority hide from our eyes.

Penal laws are the expression of the moral sentiments of mankind, and either are as variable as the other. In Holland it was once a capital offence to kill a stork, and in England to cut down a man's cherry-tree. For a Roman lady to drink wine was as heinous a sin as adultery, for either of which she incurred the extreme sentence of the law. In Athens idleness was for a long time punishable; though to a Spartan an Athenian fined for idleness seemed to be punished for keeping up his dignity. In Mexico drunkenness was a graver crime than slander; for whilst the slanderer lost his ears or lips, the drunken man or woman was clubbed or stoned to death.

But if penal laws thus express the wide variability of human morality, they also contribute to make actions moral or immoral according to the penalties by which they enforce or prevent them. For not only does whatever is immoral tend to become penal, but anything can be made immoral by being first made penal; and hence indifferent actions often remain immoral long after they have ceased to be actually punishable. Thus the Jews made Sabbath-breaking equally immoral with homicide or adultery, by affixing to each of them the same capital penalty; and the former offence, though it no longer forms part of any criminal code, has still as much moral force against it as many an offence directly punishable by the law.

But perhaps the best illustrations of the tendency of actions to retain the infamy, attached to them by a past condition of fanatical punishments, are the cases of suicide and child-killing. Could a Greek of the classical period, or a cultivated historian like Plutarch reappear on earth, nothing would strike him more vividly than the modern conception or recent treatment of these crimes. According to Plutarch, Lycurgus, the great Spartan lawgiver, met his death by voluntary starvation, from the persuasion that even the deaths of lawgivers should be of use to mankind, and serve them with an example of virtue and greatness; and Seneca held that it was the part of a wise man not to live as long as he could but as long as he ought. With what astonishment, then, would not Plutarch or Seneca read of recent European punishments for suicide—of Lady Hales losing the estate she was jointly possessed of with her husband, the Judge, because he drowned himself; of the stake and the cross-roads; of the English law which still regards suicide as murder, and condemns one of two men who in a mutual attempt at self-destruction survives the other to the punishment of the ordinary murderer! Is it possible, he would ask, that an action which was once regarded as among the noblest a man could perform, has really come to be looked upon with any other feeling than one of pity or a sad respect?

The case of infanticide suggests similar thoughts. When we remember that both Plato and Aristotle commended as a valuable social custom that which we treat as a crime; when we recall the fact that the life of a Spartan infant depended on a committee of elders, who decided whether it should live or perish, we shall better appreciate the distance we have travelled, or, as some would say, the progress we have made, if we take up some English daily paper and read of some high-minded English judge sentencing, at least formally, some wretched woman to death, because, in order to save her child from starvation or herself from shame, she has released it from existence. Yet the feeling, of which such a sentence is the expression, is often extolled as one of the highest triumphs of civilisation; and the laws, as if there were no difference between adult and infant life, glory in protecting the weakness of a child by their merciless disregard for the weakness of its mother.

But at least, it will be thought, we have by this time arrived at some principles about punishment which correspond with the eternal truths of equity. Is not Equality, for instance, one of the primary essentials of punishment? Does it not stand as a penal axiom with almost the sanction of a moral law that all men should suffer equally for equal crimes? Yet, if by equality be meant the same punishment, the same kind of labour, the same term of servitude, the same pecuniary fine—and this is the only thing it can mean—what more obvious than that the same punishment for rich and poor, for young and old, for strong and weak, for men and women, for educated and uneducated, will bring to the constitution of a penal code the utmost inequality the imagination can conceive? Beccaria insists that the law can do no more than assign the same extrinsic punishment to the same crime; that is, the same punishment, regardless of all other external considerations; and he calls for the infliction of the same punishment on the nobleman as on the commoner. Let it be so; but the same punishment is no longer an equal one; and hence from this very demand for equality springs the demand for its very opposite, for what Bentham calls the *equability* of punishment; that is, consideration for the different circumstances of individual criminals. So that the same nominal punishment not being the same real one, equality of punishment appears to be a chimera, and the law, which punishes, say, a distinguished officer less severely than it punishes a costermonger for the same crime, errs perhaps really less from actual equality than if it condemned both to precisely the same punishment.

Again, Proportion between crime and punishment seems to be another natural demand of equity. Yet it is evident that it is only approximately possible, and will vary in every age and country according to the prevalent notions of morality. Is imprisonment for a year, or imprisonment for life, or for how long, a fair and proportionate punishment for perjury? Who shall decide? Shall we submit it to the opinion of the judges? But has not Romilly left on record the story of the two men tried by two different judges for stealing some chickens, who were sentenced respectively one to imprisonment for two months, and the other to transportation? Shall we then give up all attempt at proportion and apply the same deterrent as equally efficacious against slight or grave offences? Draco, when asked why he made death the punishment for most offences that were possible, is said to have replied, 'Small ones deserve it, and I can find no greater for the gravest.' The same reasoning was for a long time that of our own law; and in Japan, where every wrong act was one of disobedience to the Emperor, and accordingly of equal value, the same penalty of death for gambling, theft, or murder, obviated all difficulties with regard to a proportion which is easier to imagine than it is to define.

Analogy between crime and punishment is another idea which, except in the case of death for death, has been relegated from the practice of most criminal laws. Yet the principle has in its favour the authority of Moses, the authority of the whole world and of all time, that punishment should, if possible, resemble the crime it punishes in kind; so that a man who blinds another should be blinded himself, he who disfigures another be disfigured himself. Thus in the old-world mythology, Theseus and Hercules inflict on the evil powers they conquer the same cruelties their victims were famous for; Termenus having his skull broken because with his own skull he broke the heads of others; and Busiris, who sacrificed others, being himself sacrificed in his turn. Both Montesquieu and Beccaria also advocate analogy in punishment, and so does Bentham to some degree; there being, indeed, few greater contrasts between the theories of the great English jurist and modern English practice than that the former should not have deprecated some suffering by burning as a penalty analogous to the crime of arson, and that he should have advised the transfixing of a forger's hand or of a calumniator's tongue by an iron instrument before the public gaze as good and efficient punishments for forgery and slander.

These are some of the difficulties of the subject, which teach us the necessity of constant open-mindedness with regard to all ideas or practices connected with criminal law. But, would we further examine our established notions, we should consider a statement from Hobbes which goes to the very root of the theory of punishment.

'In revenges or punishments,' says Hobbes, 'men ought not to look at the greatness of the evil past, but the greatness of the good to follow, whereby we are forbidden to inflict punishment with any other design than for the correction of the offender and the admonition of others.' And over and over again the same thing has been said, till it has come to be a commonplace in the philosophy of law, that the object of punishment is to reform and deter. As was once said by a great legal authority, 'We do not hang you because you stole a horse, but that horses may not be stolen.'[42] Punishment by this theory is a means to an end, not an end in itself.

Yet, supposing it were proved to-morrow that punishment fails entirely of the ends imputed to it; that, for example, the greater number of crimes are committed by criminals who have been punished already; that

42 So Seneca, *De Ira.*, i. 16: 'Nemo prudens punit quia peccatum est, sed ne peccetur. Revocari enim præterita non possunt, futura prohibentur.' Compare *ibid.*, ii. 31, and Plato, *Laws*, xi. 934 A.

for one chance of a man's reformation during his punishment there are a hundred in favour of his deterioration; and that the deterrent influence of his punishment is altogether removed by his own descriptions of it; shall we suppose for a moment that society would cease to punish, on the ground that punishment attained none of its professed ends? Would it say to the horse-stealer, 'Keep your horse, for nothing we can do to you can make you any better, nor deter others from trying to get horses in the same way?'

Or to take a stronger case. A deserter from the ranks escapes to his home, breaks into it at night, robs an infirm father of all the savings he has provided for his old age, and in a struggle for their possession so injures him that he dies. Must the law disclaim all indignation, all resentment, in the punishment it inflicts, and say to such a ruffian that it only deals hard with him in order to warn others by his example, and with the pious hope of making a good man of him in the future? If resentment is ever just, is it wrong to give it public expression? If it is natural and right in private life, why should it be a matter of shame in public life? If there is such a thing as just anger for a single man, does it become unjust when distributed among a million?

As a matter of fact the law affords a very clear proof, that its real purpose is to administer retributive justice and that punishment has no end beyond itself, by its careful apportionment of punishment to crime, by its invariable adjustment between the evil a man has done and the evil it deals out to him in return. For what purpose punish offences according to a certain scale, for what purpose stay to measure their gravity, if merely the prevention of crime is the object of punishment? Why punish a slight theft with a few months' imprisonment and a burglary with as many years? The slight theft, as easier to commit, as more tempting accordingly, should surely have a harder penalty affixed to it than a crime which, as it is more difficult, is also less probable and less in need of strong counter-inducements to restrain it. That the law never reasons in this way is because it weighs offences according to their different degrees of criminality, or, in other words, because it feels that the fair *retaliation* for the burglary is not a fair *retaliation* for the theft.

If, moreover, the prevention of crime is the chief object of punishment, why wait till the crime is committed? Why not punish before, as a certain Turk in Barbary is said to have done, who, whenever he bought a fresh Christian slave, had him forthwith suspended by his heels and bastinadoed, that the severe sense of his punishment might prevent him from committing in future the faults that should merit it?[43] Why should we ever let a man out of prison who has once entered one? Is he not then a hundred times more likely to violate the law than he was before; and is he ever more dangerous to society than when he has once suffered for the public example, and been released from the discipline that was intended to reform him? It is still true, as Goldsmith said long ago, that we send a man to prison for one crime and let him loose again ready to commit a thousand. And so it is, that of the 74,000 souls who make up our criminal classes, whilst about 34,000 of them fill our prisons and reformatories, there is still an army of 40,000 at large in our midst, whom we class as *known thieves, receivers of stolen goods*, and *suspected persons.*[44]

A child's simple philosophy of punishment therefore is after all the correct one, when it tells you without hesitation that the reason a man is punished for a bad action is simply 'because he deserves it.' The notion of desert in punishment is based entirely on feelings of the justice of resentment. So that the primary aim of legal punishment is precisely the same as may be shown historically to have been its origin, namely, the regulation by society of the wrongs of individuals. In all early laws and societies distinct traces may be seen of the transition of the *vendetta*, or right of private revenge, from the control of the person or family injured by a crime to that of the community at large. The latter at first decided only the question of guilt, whilst leaving its punishment to the pleasure of the individuals directly concerned by it. Even to this day in Turkey sentences of death for murder run as follows: So-and-so is condemned to death *at the demand of the victim's heirs*; and such sentences are sometimes directed to be carried out in their presence.[45]-By degrees the community obtained control of the punishment as well, and thus private might became public right, and the resentment of individual injuries the Retributive Justice of the State.

---

43 The same is the philosophy of the nursery-rhyme book:—
'That's Jack. Lay a stick on his back.
What's he done? I cannot say.
We'll find out to-morrow, and beat him to-day.'
So said also a more serious authority, Periander, tyrant of Corinth, sometimes counted among the Seven Wise Men of Greece: μ μ νον το ς μαρτ νοντας λλ κα το ς μ λλοντας κ λαζε. 'Punish not only those who have done wrong, but those who are going to.'

44 *Judicial Statistics*, 1878, xi.

45 White's *Three Years in Constantinople*, ii. 331.

The recognition of this regulation of resentment as the main object of punishment affords the best test for measuring its just amount. For that amount will be found to be just which is necessary; that is to say, which just suffices for the object it aims at—the satisfaction of general or private resentment. It must be so much, and no more, as will prevent individuals from preferring to take the law into their own hands and seeking to redress their own injuries. This degree can only be gathered from experience, nor is it any real objection to it, that it must obviously be somewhat arbitrary and variable. Both Wladimir I., the first Christian Czar of Russia, and Wladimir II. tried the experiment of abolishing capital punishment for murder; but the increase of murders by the *vendetta* compelled them to fall back upon the old modes of punishment.[46] Some centuries later the Empress Elizabeth successfully tried the same experiment, without the revival of the *vendetta*, the state of society having so far altered that the relations of a murdered man no longer insisted on the death of his murderer. But had Elizabeth abolished all legal punishment for murder—had she, that is, allowed no public *vendetta* of any kind—undoubtedly the *vendetta* would have become private again.

By the same rule, in the case of theft, the value of the thing stolen, with some equivalent for the trouble of its recovery, taken from the offender or made a lien on his earnings, appears to be all that justice can demand. Sir Samuel Romilly, himself second to none as a lawyer, wrote seventy years ago: 'If the restitution of the property stolen, and only a few weeks' or even but a few days' imprisonment were the unavoidable consequence of theft, no theft would ever be committed.' Yet the following sentences are taken at random from authentic English sources: three months' imprisonment for stealing a pipe, six months for stealing a penny, a twelvemonth for stealing an umbrella, five years' penal servitude for stealing some stamps from a letter, seven years for stealing twopence. In such cases the principle of vindictiveness exceeds the limits of necessity, and therefore of justice; whilst the law loses all its dignity as the expression of unimpassioned resentment.

Is it possible, then, so beforehand to apportion punishments to crimes that when a crime is committed it shall be but necessary to refer to a code and at once detect its appropriate punishment? Or must the law be general in its language, and leave a wide margin to the discretion of the judge? Beccaria would have the judicial function confined solely to the ascertainment of the fact of a crime, its punishment preordained by the

46 Pierson, *Aus Russland's Vergangenheit*, 31, 32.

law. On the other hand it is said, that it is impossible to anticipate every case that may arise; that no two cases are ever alike; that it is better to leave the nice adjustment of penalties to the wisdom and impartiality of a judge, and only limit his discretion by rules of a most expansive description.

The Chinese penal code of 1647 is probably the nearest approach to Beccaria's conception, and nothing is more marvellous than the precision with which it apportions punishments to every shade of crime, leaving no conceivable offence, of commission or omission, without its exact number of bamboo strokes, its exact pecuniary penalty, or its exact term or distance of banishment. It is impossible in this code to conceive any discretion or room for doubt left to the judicial officers beyond the discovery of the fact of an alleged crime. But what is practicable in one country is practicable in another; so that the charge so often urged against thus eliminating judicial discretion, that it is fair in theory but impossible in practice, finds itself at direct issue with the facts of actual life.[47]

But although the laws of every country thus recognise in different degrees the retributive nature of punishment, by their constant attention to its apportionment to crime, there is another corollary of the desirability of a just proportion between the two, which has never been, nor is ever likely to be, accepted: namely, that from the point of view of the public interest, which in theory is the only legal view, it is no mitigation of a crime that it is a first offence, nor any aggravation of one that it is the second.

For since the observance of some regular proportion between crime and punishment, whatever that proportion may be, constitutes the first principle of an equitable code; and since the most important thing in public morality is a fixed penal estimate for every class of crime; it is above all things desirable that the law should always adhere to such proportion and estimate, by concerning itself solely with the crime and not with the criminal. The injury to the public is precisely the same whether a criminal has broken the law for the first time or for the thousandth and first; and to punish a man more severely for his second offence than for his first, because he has been punished before, is to cast aside all regard for that

47 See Sir G. Staunton's *Penal Code of China*, lxxi. 278-9, 285, 345, 367, 381, 449, for tables apportioning punishment to different crimes according to an exact mathematical scale. There is no reason to suppose that this scale was never acted upon, even if it is not observed now, about which there is no good evidence.

due proportion between crime and punishment which is after all the chief ingredient of retributive justice, and to inflict a penalty often altogether incommensurate with the injury inflicted on the public.

For instance, the injury to the public is no greater the hundredth time a man steals a rabbit than it is the first. The public may be interested in the prevention of poaching, but it is not interested in the person of the poacher, nor in the number of times he may have broken the law. The law claims to be impersonal—to treat offences as they affect the State, not as they affect individuals; to act mechanically, coldly, and dispassionately. It has, therefore, simply to deal with the amount of injury done by each specific offence, and to affix to it its specific penalty, regardless of all matters of moral antecedents. The repetition of an offence may make its immorality the greater, but its criminality remains the same, and this only is within the province of the law.

It is the specific crime, not the fact that it is a second or third felony, which is injurious. Neither a community nor an individual suffer more from the commission of a crime by a man who commits it for the second time than from its commission by a man who has never committed it before. If two brothers are each robbed of a pound apiece on two several occasions, the one who is robbed each time by the same criminal suffers no more than the one who is robbed each time by different criminals. Still less is the public more injured in one case than in the other. Therefore the former brother is entitled for his second loss to no more restitution than the other, nor has any more claim on society for the infliction of a severer punishment on his behalf than that inflicted for the second loss of his brother.

A few stories may be taken as illustrative of thousands to indicate the mischief and travesty of justice which arises from the neglect of this principle, and from the custom of making a legal inquiry into moral antecedents.

A farm labourer, with a wife and four children, and earning eleven shillings a week, was imprisoned in the county gaol for two months for the theft of a pound of butter. Soon after his release sickness entered his home, and to supply his children's wants he again yielded to temptation and stole twelve duck's eggs. For this he was sentenced to seven years' penal servitude; or rather not for this theft, but because he had already incurred a severe punishment for a theft of some butter. The sentence was most perfectly lawful, but was it not perfectly unjust?

Almost any number of the 'Times' will illustrate the same thing. Take the account of the Middlesex Sessions of February 24, 1880. There we find the case of a man and woman sentenced to seven and five years' penal servitude respectively. What enormities had they committed? The man had stolen three-halfpence from somebody; and the woman, who was a laundress, had stolen two skirts, of the value of six shillings, from a vendor of sheep's trotters. The man had incurred previously seven years' penal servitude for a robbery with violence, and the woman had three times in her life been sentenced to imprisonment. But is it just that, because a man has been severely punished once, no rule nor measure shall be observed with him if he incur punishment again? And might not a vendor of sheep's trotters have been satisfied, without a laundress becoming a burden to the State?

It will be said, of course, that the practice of giving increased sentences where there have been previous convictions prevails all over the world and in all states of civilisation. But in that very fact lies the strength of the argument against it. By the Roman law a third case of theft, however slight, exposed a man to death.[48] By the laws of St. Louis the man who stole a thing of trifling value lost an ear the first time, a foot the second, and was hung the third. By the criminal code of Sardinia in the fifteenth century, asses were condemned to lose one ear the first time they trespassed on a field not their master's, and their second ear for a second offence. But enough of such instances. The practice is undoubtedly universal; but so at one time were ordeals and tortures. May not, then, the practice be, like them, part and parcel of a crude state of law, such as was unavoidable in its emergence to better things, but such as it is worth some effort to escape from?

There are, however, certain limitations even to the supposed universality of the custom. For the Roman jurists did not consider a re-conviction as a circumstance in itself which justified aggravation of punishment; and all that can be gathered from some fragments in the Pandects and Code is, that some particular cases of repeated crimes were punished more severely than a first offence. But they were crimes *of the same kind*; and a man whose first crime was a theft and whose second was an assault would not have incurred an aggravated penalty. It is the same to-day in the Austrian, Tuscan, and a few other codes: a second crime is

48 Farinaccius: 'Potest pro tribus furtis, quamvis minimis, pœna mortis imponi.' The philosophy of this was, that to do anything twice was the same as doing it frequently: 'Quod bis fit, frequenter fieri dicitur.'

only punished more severely as a second crime when it is of the same kind as the first, so that it would not suffice to prove simply a previous conviction for felony irrespective of the particular sort. There is also another limitation that has sometimes been recognised, for in the Roman law the rule of an increased penalty fell to the ground, if three years elapsed without offence between the punishment for one crime and the commission of a second.[49]

If it be said that a second conviction makes it necessary for society to protect itself by stronger measures against a member who thus defies its power, it may be asked whether this is not an application of exactly the same reasoning to the crimes of individuals, which as applied to the crimes of all men generally led our ancestors so far astray in the distribution of their punishments. Nothing could have been more plausible than their reasoning: 'The punishment in vogue does not diminish the crime, therefore increase the punishment.' But nothing could have been less satisfactory than the result, for with the increase of punishment that of crime went hand in hand. The same reasoning is equally plausible in the case of individuals, with the same perplexing question resulting in the end: 'How comes it that, in spite of the threatened greater punishment, the majority of criminals are yet old offenders?'

It is unhappily no mere theory, that the majority of crimes are committed precisely by those who risk most in committing them; by those, that is, who commit them with the aggravated penalty full in view. By the existing law (of which both the Criminal Code- and the Penal Servitude-Commissioners have proposed the mitigation) anyone convicted of felony after a previous conviction for felony is liable to penal servitude for life, or to imprisonment with hard labour for four years, with one or more whippings. The minimum punishment for a second conviction of felony is seven years. Yet, with the knowledge of such increased punishments before their eyes, with the full consciousness of their liabilities as old offenders, official statistics show that of both the male and female convicts in the English convict prisons *considerably more*

49 The French have two words, récidive and récidiver, to signify a relapse into crime, the word being applied as a metaphor from medicine, where it means the recurrence of a disease. In English we might adopt the word reciduous to express renewed acts of crime after punishment.

than half have incurred previous convictions.[50] Of the male convicts in 1878, 79 per cent., and of the female 89 per cent., were cases of reciduous crime. May it not, then, be argued from such a failure of the system to an error in the principle on which it rests? For is it not evident that the aggravated penalty does as little to deter as the original punishment does to reform?

But undoubtedly punishment, although in its origin and present intention vindictive, must exercise a certain preventive force against crime, and this preventive force can scarcely be estimated, for that which is prevented is, of course, not seen. But the efficiency of punishment as a deterrent is proportioned to its certainty, and there is a large element of uncertainty that can never be eliminated. For every malefactor there are two hopes: first, that he may escape detection or apprehension; secondly, that he may escape conviction. That his hopes of impunity are not without reason greater than his fears of punishment the following facts attest.

In a period of ten years, from 1867 to 1876, the total number of principal indictable offences committed in the metropolis against property—and these constitute the great majority of crimes—were 117,345. But the apprehensions for these offences were only 26,426, the convictions only 19,242. In other words, the chances against apprehension for such crimes as burglary or larceny are four to one in favour of the criminal, whilst the chances against his conviction and punishment are fully as high as six to one. When we thus find that only 16 per cent. of such crimes receive any punishment, the remaining 84 per cent. escaping it altogether, and that only 22 per cent. are even followed by apprehension, we shall the more admire the general efficacy of our criminal machinery, in which prevention by punishment plays so small a part.[51]

But punishment bears much the same relation to crime in the country at large that it does in the metropolis. Let one year be taken as a fair sample of all. The total number of indictable offences of all kinds *reported to the police* in 1877-8 was 54,065. For these offences only 24,062 persons were apprehended. Of these latter only 16,820 were held to bail or committed

50 The figures for May 1878 are: Men, 8,983; of these only 2,064 had had no previous conviction of any kind, 4,672 had had sentences short of penal servitude, and 2,247 penal servitude sentences. Of the 1,226 women, 124 had never been convicted before, 635 had had sentences short of penal servitude, 567 penal servitude sentences.—(*P.S. Report*, iii. 1170. See also ii. 206, 296, 364.)

51 *Penal Servitude Acts Commission*, 1879, vol. iii. 1195-6.

for trial; and of these again 12,473 were convicted and punished.[52] So that, though the proportion of convictions to the number of prisoners who come to trial is about 75 per cent., the proportion of convictions, that is, of punishments, to the number of crimes committed is so low as 23 per cent. Of the 54,065 crimes reported to the police in one year 41,592 were actually committed with impunity; and thus the proportion which successful crime of all sorts bears to unsuccessful is rather more than as four to one.[53] So that there is evident truth in what a good authority has said: 'Few offences comparatively are followed by detection and punishment, and with a moderate degree of cunning an offender may generally go on for a long time with but feeble checks, if not complete impunity.'[54]

Against this general uncertainty of punishment, which no severity in the law can affect or make up for, the only certainty of punishment dependent on the law is in the event of conviction. But even this certainty is of a very qualified nature, for it depends on sentiments of due proportion between a crime and its penalty, which in no two men are the same. Every increase of severity in punishment diminishes its certainty, since it holds out to a criminal fresh hopes of impunity from the clemency of his judges, prosecutors, or jury.

But there is a still further uncertainty of punishment, for it is as well known in the criminal world as elsewhere that the sentence pronounced in court is not the real sentence, and that neither penal servitude for five years nor penal servitude for life mean necessarily anything of the sort. The humanity of modern legislation insists on a remission of punishment, dependent on a convict's life in the public works prisons, in order that the element of hope may brighten his lot and perchance reform his character. This remission was at first dependent simply on his conduct, which was perhaps too generously called good where it was hard for it to be bad; now it depends on his industry and amount of work done. Yet the element of hope might be otherwise assured than by lessening the certainty of punishment, say, by associating industry or good conduct with such little privileges of diet, letter-writing, or receiving of visits,

---

52 *Judicial Statistics*, 1878, xvi. 45.

53 The same seems to be also true of France. 'Quoi de plus important que ce fait, qu'en moyenne annuelle 30,000 crimes ou délits restent impunis parce que les auteurs en sont inconnus, et 10,000 environ parce que les charges portées contre les accusés ou prévenus ont été jugées insuffisantes.'—Legoyt, *La France et l'Étranger*, i. 406.

54 Hill, *Crime*, 28.

as still shed some rays of pleasure over the monotony of felon-life. It should not be forgotten, that the Commission of 1863, which so strongly advocated the remissibility of parts of penal sentences, did so in despite of one of its principal members, against no less an authority than the Lord Chief Justice, then Sir Alexander Cockburn.[55] The very fact of the remissibility of a sentence is an admission of its excessive severity; for to say that a sentence is never carried out is to say that it need never have been inflicted.

The question, therefore, arises, Does crime depend to any appreciable extent on imprisonment at all, or on the length or shortness of sentences?

The right to ask such a question derives itself from recent experience. In 1853 the country decided to shorten terms of penal servitude as compared with those of the then expiring system of transportation, for which they were to be substituted. Four years later it was resolved to equalise terms of penal servitude with those formerly given of transportation, though transportation for seven years was still to have its equivalent in three of penal servitude. Then came the garrotting year, 1862, in consequence of which the minimum term of penal servitude was raised to five years, whilst no sentence of penal servitude, after a previous conviction of felony, was to be for less than seven years. Now again the tide has turned in favour of shorter sentences, and it is officially proposed to relinquish the latter minimum of servitude as too severe, and as leading in practice to sentences of simple imprisonment, which on the other hand are declared to be too slight.

In such a zigzag path has our penal legislation been feeling, and is still feeling, its way, with evident misgiving of that principle of repression, as false as it is old, that an increase of crime can only be met by an increase of punishment.

There seem to be three principal reasons why, under our present system, crime still keeps its general level, irrespective of all changes in our degrees of punishment.

In the first place, our public works prisons, however excellent for their material results, are so many schools of crime, where for the one honest trade a man learns by compulsion he acquires a knowledge of three or four that are dishonest. 'I have become acquainted,' says a released convict, 'with more of what is bad and evil, together with the

55 *Memorials of Millbank*, ii. 274–5.

schemes and dodges of professional thieves and swindlers, during the four years I served the Queen for nothing, than I should have done in fifty years outside the prison walls.' 'The association rooms at Dartmoor are as bad as it is possible for anything to be ... they are really class-rooms in the college of vice, where all are alike students and professors. The present system in most instances merely completes the man's vicious and criminal education, instead of in the slightest degree reforming him.'[56] It has been attempted in various ways to obviate this difficulty, by diminishing opportunities of companionship; but the real demoralisation of prison life is probably due less to the actual contact of bad men with one another than to the deadened sense of criminality which they derive from the feeling of numbers, just as from the same cause the danger of drowning is forgotten on the ice. Prisoners in gangs lose all shame of crime, just as men in armies forget their native horror of murder.

In the second place, a large proportion of the habitual criminal class is formed of weak-minded or imbecile persons, notorious for the repeated commission of petty thefts, crimes of violence and passion, and confessed to be 'not amenable to the ordinary influences of self-interest or fear of punishment.'[57] It is now proposed to separate this class of prisoners from others; but is punishment operative on them at all? Is not their proper place an asylum?

In the third place, there is the discharge from prison; and truly, if the prevention of crime be a main object of society, it is just when a man is released from prison that, from a social point of view, there would seem most reason to send him there. For even if, whilst in prison, he has learned no dishonest means of livelihood, how shall he, when out of it, set about obtaining an honest one? If temptation was too strong for him when all doors were open to him, is it likely to be less strong when most are closed? Will it not be something like a miracle, if, with two pounds paid to him on his discharge and his railway fare paid home, he eat for any considerable time the bread of honesty, and sleep the sleep of the just?

That these causes do to a great extent defeat the preventive effect of our penal laws, is proved by the tale of our criminal statistics, which reveal the fact that most of our crime is committed by those who have once

56 The author of *Five Years' Penal Servitude*. With this testimony agrees thoroughly that of the Chaplain of Parkhurst Prison (*P.S. Rep.* iii. 707–8), that of the Governor of Portland Prison (ii. 164–5), and that of the Governor of Spike Island (iii. 814–5).

57 *Penal Servitude Report*, i. 43.

been punished, and that of general crime about 77 per cent. is committed with impunity. But if so large a proportion of crimes pass unpunished altogether, it is evident that society depends much less for its general security upon its punishments than is commonly supposed. Might it not, therefore, still further relax such punishments, which are really a severe tax on the great majority of honest people for the repression of the very small proportion who constitute the dishonest part of the community?[58]

For if punishment is weak to prevent crime, it is strong to produce it, and it is scarcely open to doubt that its productive force is far greater than its preventive. Our terms of imprisonment compel more persons to enter a career of crime than they prevent from pursuing one, that being often the only resource left for those who depend on a criminal's labour. Whether in prison or the workhouse, such dependents become a charge to society; nor does it seem reasonable, that if one man under sore temptation steals a loaf, a hundred other men who do no such thing must contribute to keep, not only the prisoner himself, but his family too, in their daily bread for so long a time as it pleases the law to detain him from earning his and their necessary subsistence.

Since, therefore, there is more to fear from a punished than from an unpunished criminal, there is the less reason to regret the general impunity of crime. There is indeed a large class of crimes for the prevention of which more would be done, by leaving them to their natural consequences, and to the strong power against them which the general interests and moral feelings of mankind will always enforce, than by actual punishment. It is particularly crimes of dishonesty which are best punished by the mere fact of their discovery. By the Norwegian law if an offender holds any official place he is punished, not by fine or imprisonment, but by the loss of his office and all the privileges connected with it.[59] And if we imagine a country without any legal penalty at all for theft or dishonesty, thieves and their tribe would soon find their proper punishment, by that process of social shifting, which would drive them to the most deleterious or dangerous occupations of life even more effectually than it so drives them at present. The less dependence is placed on the penal sanctions of crime, the stronger do the moral restraints from it become.

58 If we include offences proceeded against summarily with the indictable offences reported, about 2 per cent. of the population may be counted as dishonest.

59 *Strafgesetzbuch*, c. vi. 33.

It is against crimes affecting the person that punishments are most desirable and their vindictive character most justly displayed. Personal violence calls for personal detention or personal chastisement; and the principle of analogy in punishment is most appropriate in the case of a man who maltreats his wife or abuses his strength against any weakness greater than his own. Punishment in such cases is a demand of natural justice, whether anyone is affected by the example or not, and whether or not the man himself is improved by it. Not only is it the best means of enforcing that personal security which is one of the main functions of the State, but it is an expression of that sense of moral reprobation which is so necessary to the good order of society.

Repression by the law seems likewise the only means of preventing that large class of actions which affect the general character and tone of a country, whilst they injuriously affect no individual in particular. The protection of creatures too feeble to protect themselves justifies, under this head, the legal punishment of cruelty to animals. It is idle to say that the law can do nothing against the average moral sense of the community, for the law is often at first the only possible lever of our moral ideas. Were it not for the law we should still bait bulls and bears, and find amusement in cock-throwing; and till the law includes hares and pigeons within the pale of protection drawn so tenderly round bulls and bears, no moral sense is likely to arise against the morbid pleasures of coursing and pigeon-shooting.

That the punishments of long custody by which we now defend our lives and properties are out of all proportion to the real needs of social existence is indicated by such a fact as that no increase of crime used to attend the periodical release of prisoners which was for long, if it is not still, customary in Russia at the beginning of each reign. Neither in India, when on the Queen's assumption of the title of Empress, a pardon was granted to about one-tenth of the prison population, did any increase of crime ensue, as, according to all criminal reasoning, it should have done, if the safety of society depends on the custody of the criminal class.[60] In Sweden a low rate of crime seems to be a direct consequence of a low scale of punishment. Of those condemned to *travaux forcés*, which may vary from a period of two months to a period for life, 64 per cent. are condemned for one year, and only 3 per cent. are condemned for seven

60 Wheeler, *Imperial Assemblage at Delhi*, 1877, 124, 127.

years;[61] whilst sentences to the latter period in England form between 50 and 60 per cent. of the sentences to penal servitude.

But if the custody of the criminal class has been overrated as a preventive of crime, or regarded as the sole preventive instead of one amongst many, it does not follow that crime on that account must be left to itself. It only follows that we should trust to punishment less and to other agencies more in our war with crime, and that we should seek to check the latter at its source, not in its full stream, by attending to the improvement of the general conditions of life. It is quite certain, for instance, that the spread of education, of which Beccaria wrote in terms of such despair, means the diminution of crime; and as the majority of crimes are committed between the ages of twenty and forty, it may be predicted that from the present year onwards the great Act of 1870 will bear increasing fruit in lowering our criminal statistics. More too may be hoped for from the electric light than from any multiplication of prisons.

There are a few obvious remedies by which the inducements to crime might be easily diminished. In 1808 Sir Samuel Romilly brought in a bill, to provide persons tried and acquitted of felony with compensation, at the discretion of the judge, for the loss they incurred by their detention and trial. This was objected to, on the ground that the payment of such compensation out of the county rates would discourage prosecutions; and the only justice done to men falsely accused from that day to this is the authorisation given to goal-governors in 1878 to provide prisoners, who have been brought from another county for trial at the assizes and have been acquitted, with means of returning to their own homes. Something more than this is required to save a man so situated from falling into real crime.

One thing that might be done, which would also serve at the same time to keep a prisoner's family from want, the main source of crime, would be the formation of a Prisoners' Fund, for his and their benefit. For this there is a precedent in a quite recent Act. For the Act, which abolished the forfeiture of a felon's property, enabled the Crown to appoint an administrator of it, for the benefit of the persons injured by the crime and the felon's family, the property itself and its income reverting ultimately to the convict or to his representatives. There could, however, be no objection in justice to the forfeiture of a proportionate part of every felon's property, such forfeiture to be dedicated to the formation of a fund, out of which assistance should be given, both to the families of prisoners

61 *Congrès pénitentiaire international.* Tableau xii.

during their custody and to the prisoners themselves on their discharge.[62] Such a fund might be still further increased by the substitution of a lien on a man's wages or income for many minor offences now punished, but not prevented, by imprisonment.

By the present English law a person convicted of more offences than one may be sentenced for each offence separately, the punishment of each one in succession taking effect on the expiration of the other. By this law (which the Criminal Code Commissioners propose to alter) imprisonment may be spread over the whole of a lifetime. On this point the Chinese law again offers a model, for it enacts that when two or more offences are proved against a man, they shall all be estimated together, and the punishment of all the lesser offences be included in that of the principal charge, not in addition to it So also if the offences are charged at different times, and the punishment of one has been already discharged, there is no further punishment for the other subsequent charges, unless they be charges of greater criminality, in which case only the difference between the punishments can be legally incurred.[63] But this of course presupposes a definite scale of crimes and punishments.

Such are some of the problems connected with penology, which best illustrate the imperfection of its hitherto attained results. Only one thing as yet seems to stand out from the mist, which is, that closely associated as crime and punishment are both in thought and speech, they are but little associated in reality. The amount of crime in a country appears to be a given quantity, dependent on quite other causes than the penal laws directed to its repression. The efficiency of the latter seems proportioned to their mildness, not to their severity; such severity being always spoiled by an inevitable moderation in practice. The conclusion, therefore, would seem to be, that a short simple code, with every punishment attached to every offence, with every motive for aggravation of punishment stated, and on so moderate a scale that no discretion for its mitigation should be necessary, would be the means best calculated to give to penal laws their utmost value as preventives of crime, though experience proves that as such preventives their place is a purely secondary one in a really good system of legislation.

62 There is a precedent for such a law in the legislation of Leopold, Grand Duke of Tuscany: 'Les malheureux injustement emprisonnés et reconnus innocents devaient être indemnisés au moyen d'un fonds formé par les amendes, mésure équitable et profondément humaine.'—LOISELEUR, *Hist. des Peines*, 336.

63 Staunton's *Penal Code of China*, 29.

DEI DELITTI E DELLE PENE

By The

MARQUIS CESARE BECCARIA

Translated

'In rebus quibuscumque difficilioribus non expectandum ut quis simul et serat et metat, sed præparatione opus est, ut per gradus maturescant.'—BACON.

TO THE READER

Some remnants of the laws of an ancient conquering people, which a prince who reigned in Constantinople some 1,200 years ago caused to be compiled, mixed up afterwards with Lombard rites and packed in the miscellaneous volumes of private and obscure commentators—these are what form that set of traditional opinions which from a great part of Europe receive nevertheless the name of laws; and to this day it is a fact, as disastrous as it is common, that some opinion of Carpzovius, some old custom pointed out by Clarus, or some form of torture suggested in terms of complacent ferocity by Farinaccius, constitute the laws, so carelessly followed by those, who in all trembling ought to exercise their government over the lives and fortunes of men. These laws, the dregs of the most barbarous ages, are examined in this book in so far as regards criminal jurisprudence, and I have dared to expose their faults to the directors of the public happiness in a style which may keep at a distance the unenlightened and intolerant multitude. The spirit of frank inquiry after truth, of freedom from commonplace opinions, in which this book is written, is a result of the mild and enlightened Government under which the Author lives. The great monarchs, the benefactors of humanity, who are now our rulers, love the truths expounded, with force but without fanaticism, by the obscure philosopher, who is only roused to indignation by the excesses of tyranny, but is restrained by reason; and existing abuses, for whosoever well studies all the circumstances, are the satire and reproach of past ages, and by no means of the present age or of its lawgivers.

Whoever, therefore, shall wish to honour me with his criticisms, I would have begin with a thorough comprehension of the purpose of my work—a purpose which, so far from diminishing legitimate authority, will serve to increase it, if opinion can effect more over men's minds than force, and if the mildness and humanity of the government shall justify it in the eyes of all men. The ill-conceived criticisms that have been published against this book are founded on confused notions, and compel me to interrupt for a moment the arguments I was addressing to my enlightened readers, in order to close once for all every door against the misapprehensions of timid bigotry or against the calumnies of malice and envy.

There are three sources of the moral and political principles which govern mankind, namely, revelation, natural law, and social conventions. With regard to their principal object there is no comparison between the first and the other two, but they all resemble one another in this, that they all three conduce to the happiness of this present mortal life. To consider the different relations of social conventions is not to exclude those of revelation and natural law; rather it is the thousandfold changes which revelation and natural law, divine and immutable though they be, have undergone in the depraved mind of man, by his own fault, owing to false religions and arbitrary notions of virtue and vice, that make it appear necessary to examine, apart from all other considerations, the result of purely human conventions, expressed or implied, for the public need and welfare: this being an idea in which every sect and every moral system must necessarily agree; and it will always be a laudable endeavour, which seeks to constrain the headstrong and unbelieving to conform to the principles that induce men to live together in society. There are, then, three distinct kinds of virtue and vice—the religious, the natural, and the political. These three kinds ought never to conflict, although all the consequences and duties that flow from any one of them do not necessarily flow from the others. The natural law does not require all that revelation requires, nor does the purely social law require all that natural law requires; but it is most important to distinguish the consequences of the conventional law—that is, of the express or tacit agreements among men—from the consequences of the natural law or of revelation, because therein lies the limit of that power, which can rightly be exercised between man and man without a special mandate from the Supreme Being. Consequently the idea of political virtue may, without any slur upon it, be said to be variable; that of natural virtue would be always clear and manifest, were it not obscured by the stupidity or the passions of men; whilst the idea of religious virtue remains ever one and the same, because revealed directly from God and by Him preserved.

It would, therefore, be a mistake to ascribe to one, who only discusses social conventions and their consequences, principles contrary either to natural law or to revelation, for the reason that he does not discuss them. It would be a mistake, when he speaks of a state of war as anterior to a state of society, to understand it in the sense of Hobbes, as meaning that no obligation nor duty is prior to the existence of society, instead of understanding it as a fact due to the corruption of human nature and the want of any expressed sanction. It would be a mistake to impute it as a fault to a writer who is considering the results of the social compact that he does not admit them as pre-existent to the formation of the compact itself.

Divine justice and natural justice are in their essence immutable and constant, because the relation between similar things is always the same; but human or political justice, being nothing more than a relation between a given action and a given state of society, may vary according as such action becomes necessary or useful to society; nor is such justice easily discernible, save by one who analyses the complex and very changeable relations of civil combinations. When once these principles, essentially distinct, become confused, there is no more hope of sound reasoning about public matters. It appertains to the theologian to fix the boundaries between the just and the unjust, in so far as regards the intrinsic goodness or wickedness of an act; to fix the relations between the politically just and unjust appertains to the publicist; nor can the one object cause any detriment to the other, when it is obvious how the virtue that is purely political ought to give place to that immutable virtue which emanates from God.

Whoever, then, I repeat, will honour me with his criticisms, let him not begin by supposing me to advocate principles destructive of virtue or religion, seeing that I have shown that such are not my principles; and instead of his proving me to be an infidel or a rebel, let him contrive to find me a bad reasoner or a shortsighted politician; but let him not tremble at every proposition on behalf of the interests of humanity; let him convince me either of the inutility or of the possible political mischief of my principles; let him prove to me the advantage of received practices. I have given a public testimony of my religion and of my submission to my sovereign in my reply to the Notes and Observations; to reply to other writings of a similar nature would be superfluous; but whoever will write with that grace which becomes honest men, and with that knowledge which shall relieve me from the proof of first principles, of what character soever, he shall find in me not so much a man who is eager to reply as a peaceable lover of the truth.

CHAPTER I

Introduction

Men for the most part leave the regulation of their chief concerns to the prudence of the moment, or to the discretion of those whose interest it is to oppose the wisest laws; such laws, namely, as naturally help to diffuse the benefits of life, and check that tendency they have to accumulate in the hands of a few, which ranges on one side the extreme of power and happiness, and on the other all that is weak and wretched. It is only, therefore, after having passed through a thousand errors in matters that most nearly touch their lives and liberties, only after weariness of evils that have been suffered to reach a climax, that men are induced to seek a remedy for the abuses which oppress them, and to recognise the clearest truths, which, precisely on account of their simplicity, escape the notice of ordinary minds, unaccustomed as they are to analyse things, and apt to receive their impressions anyhow, from tradition rather than from inquiry.

We shall see, if we open histories, that laws, which are or ought to be covenants between free men, have generally been nothing but the instrument of the passions of some few men, or the result of some accidental and temporary necessity. They have never been dictated by an unimpassioned student of human nature, able to concentrate the actions of a multitude of men to a single point of view, and to consider them from that point alone—*the greatest happiness divided among the greatest number.* Happy are those few nations which have not waited for the slow movement of human combinations and changes to cause an approach to better things, after intolerable evils, but have hastened the intermediate steps by good laws; and deserving is that philosopher of the gratitude of mankind, who had the courage, from the obscurity of his despised study, to scatter abroad among the people the first seeds, so long fruitless, of useful truths.

The knowledge of the true relations between a sovereign and his subjects, and of those between different nations; the revival of commerce by the light of philosophical truths, diffused by printing; and the silent international war of industry, the most humane and the most worthy of rational men—these are the fruits which we owe to the enlightenment of this century. But how few have examined and combated the cruelty of punishments, and the irregularities of criminal procedures, a part of legislation so elementary and yet so neglected in almost the whole of Europe; and how few have sought, by a return to first principles, to dissipate the mistakes accumulated by many centuries, or to mitigate, with at least that force which belongs only to ascertained truths, the excessive caprice of ill-directed power, which has presented up to this time but one long example of lawful and cold-blooded atrocity! And yet the groans of the weak, sacrificed to the cruelty of the ignorant or to the indolence of the rich; the barbarous tortures, multiplied with a severity as useless as it is prodigal, for crimes either not proved or quite chimerical; the disgusting horrors of a prison, enhanced by that which is the cruellest executioner of the miserable—namely, uncertainty;—these ought to startle those rulers whose function it is to guide the opinion of men's minds.

The immortal President, Montesquieu, has treated cursorily of this matter; and truth, which is indivisible, has forced me to follow the luminous footsteps of this great man; but thinking men, for whom I write, will be able to distinguish my steps from his. Happy shall I esteem myself if, like him, I shall succeed in obtaining the secret gratitude of the unknown and peaceable followers of reason, and if I shall inspire them with that pleasing thrill of emotion with which sensitive minds respond to the advocate of the interests of humanity.

To examine and distinguish all the different sorts of crimes and the manner of punishing them would now be our natural task, were it not that their nature, which varies with the different circumstances of times and places, would compel us to enter upon too vast and wearisome a mass of detail. But it will suffice to indicate the most general principles and the most pernicious and common errors, in order to undeceive no less those who, from a mistaken love of liberty, would introduce anarchy, than those who would be glad to reduce their fellow-men to the uniform regularity of a convent.

What will be the penalty suitable for such and such crimes?

Is death a penalty really *useful and necessary* for the security and good order of society?

Are torture and torments *just*, and do they attain the *end* which the law aims at?

What is the best way of preventing crimes?

Are the same penalties equally useful in all times?

What influence have they on customs?

These problems deserve to be solved with such geometrical precision as shall suffice to prevail over the clouds of sophistication, over seductive eloquence, or timid doubt. Had I no other merit than that of having been the first to make clearer to Italy that which other nations have dared to write and are beginning to practise, I should deem myself fortunate; but if, in maintaining the rights of men and of invincible truth, I should contribute to rescue from the spasms and agonies of death any unfortunate victim of tyranny or ignorance, both so equally fatal, the blessings and tears of a single innocent man in the transports of his joy would console me for the contempt of mankind.

CHAPTER II

The Origin of Punishments—The Right of Punishment

From political morality, unless founded on the immutable sentiments of mankind, no lasting advantage can be hoped. Whatever law deviates from these sentiments will encounter a resistance which will ultimately prevail over it, just in the same way as a force, however slight, if constantly applied, will prevail over a violent motion applied to any physical body.

If we consult the human heart we shall therein discover the fundamental principles of the real right of the sovereign to punish crimes.

No man has gratuitously parted with a portion of his own liberty with a view to the public good; that is a chimera which only exists in romances. Each one of us would wish, if it were possible, that the covenants which bind others should not bind himself. There is no man but makes himself the central object of all the combinations of the globe.

The multiplication of the human race, slight in the abstract, but far in excess of the means afforded by nature, barren and deserted as it originally was, for the satisfaction of men's ever increasing wants, caused the first savages to associate together. The first unions necessarily led to others to oppose them, and so the state of war passed from individuals to nations.

Laws are the conditions under which men, leading independent and isolated lives, joined together in society, when tired of living in a perpetual state of war, and of enjoying a liberty which the uncertainty of its tenure rendered useless. Of this liberty they voluntarily sacrificed a part, in order to enjoy the remainder in security and quiet. The sum-total of all these portions of liberty, sacrificed for the good of each individually, constitutes the sovereignty of a nation, and the sovereign is the lawful trustee and administrator of these portions. But, besides forming this trust-fund, or deposit, it was necessary to protect it from the encroachments of individuals, whose aim it ever is not only to recover from the fund their own deposit, but to avail themselves of that contributed by others. 'Sensible motives,' were therefore wanted to divert the despotic will of the individual from re-plunging into their primitive chaos the laws of society. Such motives were found in punishments, established against transgressors of the laws; and I call them *sensible* motives, because experience has shown that the majority of men adopt no fixed rules of conduct, nor avoid that universal principle of dissolution, observable alike in the moral as in the physical world, save by reason of motives which directly strike the senses and constantly present themselves to the mind, counterbalancing the strong impressions of private passions, opposed as they are to the general welfare; not eloquence, nor declamations, nor the most sublime truths have ever sufficed to curb the passions for any length of time, when excited by the lively force of present objects.

As it, then, was necessity which constrained men to yield a part of their individual liberty, it is certain that each would only place in the general deposit the least possible portion—only so much, that is, as would suffice to induce others to defend it. The aggregate of these least possible portions constitutes the right of punishment; all that is beyond this is an abuse and not justice, a fact but not a right.[64] Punishments which exceed what is necessary to preserve the deposit of the public safety are in their nature unjust; and the more just punishments are, the more sacred and inviolable is personal security, and the greater the liberty that the sovereign preserves for his subjects.

---

64 Note that the word Right is not opposed to the word Force; but the former is rather a modification of the latter; that is, the modification most advantageous to the greater number. And by justice I mean nothing else than the chain which is necessary for holding together private interests and preventing their breaking away into the original state of insociability.

One must be careful not to attach to this word Justice the idea of anything real, as of a physical force or an independent entity; it is only a human mode of thinking, a mode that has unbounded influence over each one's happiness. Still less do I mean that other kind of justice that has emanated from God, and has its immediate connection with the penalties and rewards of a future life.

CHAPTER III

Consequences

The first consequence of these principles is, that the laws alone can decree punishments for crimes, and this authority can only rest with the legislator, who represents collective society as united by a social contract. No magistrate (who is part of society) can justly inflict punishments upon another member of the same society. But since a punishment that exceeds the legally fixed limit is the lawful punishment *plus* another one, a magistrate can, under no pretext of zeal or the public good, add to the penalty already decreed against a delinquent citizen.

The second consequence is, that the sovereign, who represents society itself, can only form general laws, obligatory on all; he cannot judge whether any one in particular has broken the social compact, for in that case the nation would be divided into two parties, one represented by the sovereign, asserting the violation of such contract; the other by the accused, denying the same. Hence the necessity of a third person to judge of the fact; in other words, of a magistrate, whose decisions shall simply consist of affirmations or denials of particular facts, and shall also be subject to no appeal.

The third consequence is this: if it were proved that the severity of punishments were simply useless (to say nothing of being directly opposed to the public good and to the very object of preventing crimes), even in that case it would be contrary not only to those beneficent virtues that flow from an enlightened reason, which prefers to rule over happy human beings than over a flock of slaves, the constant victims of timid cruelty, but it would be also contrary to justice and to the nature of the social contract itself.

CHAPTER IV

Interpretation of The Laws

There is also a fourth consequence of the above principles: that the right to interpret penal laws cannot possibly rest with the criminal judges, for the very reason that they are not legislators. The judges have not received the laws from our ancestors as a family tradition, as a legacy that only left to posterity the duty of obeying them, but they receive them from living society, or from the sovereign that represents it and is the lawful trustee of the actual result of men's collective wills; they receive them, not as obligations arising from an ancient oath[65] (null, because it bound wills not then in existence, and iniquitous, because it reduced men from a state of society to that of a flock), but as the result of the tacit or expressed oath made to the sovereign by the united wills of living subjects, as chains necessary for curbing and regulating the disorders caused by private interests. This is the natural and real source of the authority of the laws.

Who, then, will be the rightful interpreter of the laws? Will it be the sovereign, the trustee of the actual wills of all, or the judge, whose sole function it is to examine whether such and such a man has committed an illegal act or not?

In every criminal case a judge ought to form a complete syllogistic deduction, in which the statement of the general law constitutes the *major premiss*; the conformity or non-conformity of a particular action with the law, the *minor premiss*; and acquittal or punishment, the conclusion. When

65 If every individual is bound to society, society is no less bound to every individual by a contract which is necessarily obligatory on both sides. This obligation, which descends from the throne to the cabin, which binds equally the greatest and most miserable of men, means nothing but that it is the interest of all men that covenants advantageous to the greater number should be observed

The word 'obligation' is one of those which are much more frequent in ethics than in any other science, and which are the abbreviated symbol of a train of reasoning rather than of a single idea. Seek for an idea corresponding to the word 'obligation' and you will seek in vain; reason about it, and you will both understand yourself and be understood by others..

a judge is obliged, or of his own accord wishes, to make even no more than two syllogisms, the door is opened to uncertainty.

Nothing is more dangerous than that common axiom, 'We must consult the spirit of the laws.' It is like breaking down a dam before the torrent of opinions. This truth, which seems a paradox to ordinary minds, more struck as they are by a little present inconvenience than by the pernicious but remote consequences which flow from a false principle enrooted among a people, seems to me to be demonstrated. Our knowledge and all our ideas are reciprocally connected together; and the more complicated they are, the more numerous are the approaches to them, and the points of departure. Every man has his own point of view—a different one at different times; so that 'the spirit of the laws' would mean the result of good or bad logic on the part of a judge, of an easy or difficult digestion; it would depend now on the violence of his passions, now on the feebleness of the sufferer, on the relationship between the judge and the plaintiff, or on all those minute forces which change the appearances of everything in the fluctuating mind of man. Hence it is that we see a citizen's fate change several times in his passage from one court to another; that we see the lives of wretches at the mercy of the false reasonings or of the temporary caprice of a judge, who takes as his rightful canon of interpretation the vague result of all that confused series of notions which affect his mind. Hence it is that we see the same crimes punished differently by the same court at different times, owing to its having consulted, not the constant and fixed voice of the laws, but their unstable and erring interpretations.

No inconvenience that may arise from a strict observance of the letter of penal laws is to be compared with the inconveniences of subjecting them to interpretation. The momentary inconvenience in the former case involves, indeed, correcting the words of the law which are the cause of the uncertainty, a task both easy and necessary; but the fatal licence of arguing, the source of so many arbitrary and venal disputes, is thereby prevented. When a fixed code of laws, which must be observed to the letter, leaves to the judge no further trouble than to inquire into the actions of citizens and to decide on their conformity to the written law; when the standard of just and unjust, which should equally direct the actions of the ignorant citizen as of the philosophical one, is not a matter of controversy but of fact; then are people no longer subject to the petty tyrannies of many men, which are all the more cruel by reason of the smaller distance that separates the sufferer from the inflictor of suffering, and which are more pernicious than the tyrannies of a single man, inasmuch as the despotism of many is only curable by that of one, and a despot's cruelty is proportioned, not to the power he possesses, but to the obstacles he encounters. Under a fixed code of laws citizens acquire that consciousness of personal security, which is just, because it is the object of social existence, and which is useful, because it enables them to calculate exactly the evil consequences of a misdeed. It is true they will also acquire a spirit of independence, but not such a spirit as will seek to shake the laws and prove rebellious against the chief magistrates, except against such of them as have dared to apply the sacred name of virtue to a spiritless submission to their own self-interested and capricious opinions. These principles will displease those who have assumed the right to transfer to their subordinates the strokes of tyranny they themselves have suffered from their superiors. I personally should have everything to fear, if the spirit of tyranny and the spirit of reading ever went together.

CHAPTER V

Obscurity of The Laws

If the interpretation of laws is an evil, it is clear that their obscurity, which necessarily involves interpretation, must be an evil also, and an evil which will be at its worst where the laws are written in any other than the vernacular language of a country. For in that case the people, being unable to judge of themselves how it may fare with their liberty or their limbs, are made dependent on a small class of men; and a book, which should be sacred and open to all, becomes, by virtue of its language, a private and, so to speak, a family manual.

The greater the number of those who understand and have in their hands the sacred code of the laws, the fewer will be the crimes committed; for it is beyond all doubt that ignorance and uncertainty of punishments lend assistance to the eloquence of the passions. Yet what shall we think of mankind, when we reflect, that such a condition of the laws is the inveterate custom of a large part of cultivated and enlightened Europe?

One consequence of these last reflections is, that without writing no society will ever assume a fixed form of government, wherein the power shall belong to the social whole, and not to its parts, and wherein the laws, only alterable by the general will, shall not suffer corruption in their passage through the crowd of private interests. Experience and reason have taught us, that the probability and certainty of human traditions diminish in proportion to their distance from their source. So that if there be no standing memorial of the social contract, how will laws ever resist the inevitable force of time and passion?

From this we see how useful is the art of printing, which makes the public, and not a few individuals, the guardians of the sacred laws, and which has scattered that dark spirit of cabal and intrigue, destined to disappear before knowledge and the sciences, which, however apparently despised, are in reality feared by those that follow in their wake. This is the reason that we see in Europe the diminution of those atrocious crimes that afflicted our ancestors and rendered them by turns tyrants or slaves.

Whoever knows the history of two or three centuries ago and of our own, can see that from the lap of luxury and effeminacy have sprung the most pleasing of all human virtues, humanity, charity, and the toleration of human errors; he will know what have been the results of that which is so wrongly called 'old-fashioned simplicity and honesty.' Humanity groaning under implacable superstition; the avarice and ambition of a few dyeing with human blood the golden chests and thrones of kings; secret assassinations and public massacres; every noble a tyrant to the people; the ministers of the Gospel truth polluting with blood hands that every day came in contact with the God of mercy—these are not the works of this enlightened age, which some, however, call corrupt.

CHAPTER VI

Imprisonment

An error, not less common than it is contrary to the object of society—that is, to the consciousness of personal security—is leaving a magistrate to be the arbitrary executor of the laws, free at his pleasure to imprison a citizen, to deprive a personal enemy of his liberty on frivolous pretexts, or to leave a friend unpunished in spite of the strongest proofs of his guilt. Imprisonment is a punishment which, unlike every other, must of necessity precede the declaration of guilt; but this distinctive character does not deprive it of the other essential of punishment, namely, that the law alone shall determine the cases under which it shall be merited. It is for the law, therefore, to point out the amount of evidence of a crime which shall justify the detention of the accused, and his subjection to examination and punishment. For such detention there may be sufficient proofs in common report, in a man's flight, in a non-judicial confession, or in the confession of an accomplice; in a man's threats against or constant enmity with the person injured; in all the facts of the crime, and similar indications. But these proofs should be determined by the laws, not by the judges, whose decisions, when they are not particular applications of a general maxim in a public code, are always adverse to political liberty. The more that punishments are mitigated, that misery and hunger are banished from prisons, that pity and mercy are admitted within their iron doors, and are set above the inexorable and hardened ministers of justice, the slighter will be the evidences of guilt requisite for the legal detention of the suspected.

A man accused of a crime, imprisoned and acquitted, ought to bear no mark of disgrace. How many Romans, accused of the gravest crimes and then found innocent, were reverenced by the people and honoured with magisterial positions! For what reason, then, is the lot of a man innocently accused so different in our own times? Because, in the criminal system now in vogue, the idea of force and might is stronger in men's minds than the idea of justice; because accused and convicted are thrown in confusion into the same dungeon; because imprisonment is rather a man's punishment than his mere custody; and because the two forces which should be united are separated from one another, namely, the internal force, which protects the laws, and the external force, which defends the throne and the nation. Were they united, the former, through the common sanction of the laws, would possess in addition a judicial capacity, although independent of that possessed by the supreme judicial power; and the glory that accompanies the pomp and ceremony of a military body would remove the infamy, which, like all popular sentiments, is more attached to the manner than the thing, as is proved by the fact that military prisons are not regarded in public estimation as so disgraceful as civil ones. There still remain among our people, in their customs and in their laws (always a hundred years, in point of merit, in arrear of the actual enlightenment of a nation), there still remain, I say, the savage impressions and fierce ideas of our ancestors of the North.

CHAPTER VII

Proofs and Forms of Judgment

There is a general theorem which is most useful for calculating the certainty of a fact, as, for instance, the force of the proofs in the case of a given crime:—

1. When the proofs of a fact are dependent one on another—that is to say, when each single proof rests on the weight of some other—then the more numerous the proofs are, the smaller is the probability of the fact in question, because the chances of error in the preliminary proofs would increase the probability of error in the succeeding ones.

2. When the proofs of a fact all depend equally on a single one, their number neither increases nor diminishes the probability of the fact in question, because their total value resolves itself into that of the single one on which they depend.

3. When the proofs are independent of each other—that is to say, when they do not derive their value one from the other—then the more numerous the proofs adduced, the greater is the probability of the fact in question, because the falsity of one proof affects in no way the force of another.

I speak of probability in connection with crimes, which, to deserve punishment, ought to be proved. But the paradox is only apparent, if one reflects that, strictly speaking, moral certainty is only a probability, but a probability which is called certainty, because every sensible person necessarily assents to it, by a force of habit which arises from the necessity of acting, and which is prior to all speculation. The certainty requisite for certifying that a man is a criminal is, therefore, the same that determines everyone in the most important actions of his life. The proofs of a crime may be divided into 'perfect' and 'imperfect,' the former being of such a nature as exclude the possibility of a man's innocence, and the latter such as fall short of this certainty. Of the first kind one proof alone is sufficient for condemnation; of the second, or imperfect kind, as many are necessary as suffice to make a single perfect proof; that is to say, when, though each proof taken separately does not exclude the possibility of innocence, yet their convergence on the same point makes such innocence impossible. But let it be noted that imperfect proofs, from which an accused has it in his power to justify himself and declines to do so, become perfect. This moral certainty of proofs, however, is easier to feel than to define with exactitude: for which reason I think that the best law is one which attaches to the chief judge assessors, taken by lot, not by selection, there being in this case more safety in the ignorance which judges by sentiment than in the knowledge which judges by opinion. Where the laws are clear and precise, the function of a judge consists solely in the certification of fact. If for searching out the proofs of a crime ability and cleverness are required, and if in the presentation of the result clearness and precision are essential, all that is required to judge of the result is simple and common good sense, a faculty which is less fallacious than the learning of a judge, accustomed as he is to wish to find men guilty and to reduce everything to an artificial system borrowed from his studies. Happy the nation where the laws are not a science! It is a most useful law that everyone shall be judged by his equals, because where a citizen's liberty and fortune are at stake those sentiments which inequality inspires should have no voice; that feeling of superiority with which the prosperous man regards the unfortunate one, and that feeling of dislike with which an inferior regards his superior, have no scope in a judgment by one's equals. But when the crime in question is an offence against a person of a different rank from the accused, then one half of the judges should be the equals of the accused, the other half equals of the plaintiff, that so, every private interest being balanced, by which the appearances of things are involuntarily modified, only the voice of the laws and of truth may be heard. It is also in accordance with justice that an accused person should have power up to a certain point of refusing judges whom he may suspect; and if he is allowed the exercise of this power for some time without opposition, he will seem to condemn himself. Verdicts should be public, and the proofs of guilt public, in order that opinion—which is, perhaps, the only bond of society there is—may place a check on outbursts of force and passion, and that the people may say, 'We are not slaves without defence': a feeling which both inspires them with courage and is as good as a tribute to a sovereign who understands his real interest. I refrain from pointing out other details and precautions which require similar regulations. I should have said nothing at all, had it been necessary for me to say everything.

CHAPTER VIII

Witnesses

It is a great point in every good system of laws to determine exactly the credibility of witnesses and the proofs of guilt Every reasonable man—that is, every man with a certain connection between his ideas and with feelings like those of other men—is capable of bearing witness. The true measure of his credibility is only the interest he has in speaking or in not speaking the truth; so that nothing can be more frivolous than to reject the evidence of women on the pretext of their feebleness, nothing more childish than to apply the results of real death to civil death as regards the testimony of the condemned, nothing more unmeaning than to insist on the mark of infamy in the infamous when they have no interest in lying.

Among other abuses of grammar, which have no slight influence on human affairs, that one is notable which makes the evidence of a condemned criminal null and void. 'He is *dead civilly*' say gravely the peripatetic lawyers, 'and a *dead man* is incapable of any action.' In support of this silly metaphor many victims have been sacrificed, and it has very often been disputed with all seriousness whether the truth should not yield to judicial formulas. Provided that the testimony of a condemned criminal does not go to the extent of stopping the course of justice, why should not a fitting period be allowed, even after condemnation, both to the extreme wretchedness of the criminal and to the interests of truth, so that, by his adducing fresh matter to alter the complexion of the fact, he may justify himself or others in a new trial? Forms and ceremonies are necessary in the administration of justice, because they leave nothing to the free will of the administrator; because they give the people an idea of a justice which is not tumultuary and self-interested, but steadfast and regular; and because men, the slaves of habit and imitation, are more influenced by their feelings than by arguments. But such forms can never without fatal danger be so firmly fixed by the laws as to be injurious to truth, which from being either too simple or two complex needs some external pomp to conciliate the ignorant populace.

The credibility, therefore, of a witness must diminish in proportion to the hatred, friendship, or close connection between himself and the accused. More than one witness is necessary, because, so long as one affirms and another denies, nothing is proved, and the right which everyone has of being held innocent prevails. The credibility of a witness becomes appreciably less, the greater the atrocity of the crime imputed,[66] or the improbability of the circumstances, as in charges of magic and gratuitously cruel actions. It is more likely, as regards the former accusation, that many men should lie than that such an accusation should be true, because it is easier for many men to be united in an ignorant mistake or in persecuting hatred than for one man to exercise a power which God either has not conferred or has taken away from every created being. The same reasoning holds good also of the second accusation, for man is only cruel in proportion to his interest to be so, to his hatred or to his fear. Properly speaking, there is no superfluous feeling in human nature, every feeling being always in strict accordance with the impressions made upon the senses. In the same way the credibility of a witness may sometimes be lessened by the fact of his being a member of some secret society, whose purposes and principles are either not well understood or differ from those of general acceptance; for such a man has not only his own passions but those of others besides.

Lastly, a witness's evidence is almost null when spoken words are construed into a crime. For the tone, the gesture, all that precedes or follows the different ideas attached by men to the same words, so alter

66 According to the criminalists the greater the atrocity of the crime the greater the credibility of the witness. Look at the iron maxim dictated by the most cruel stupidity: *In atrocissimis leviores conjecture sufficiunt, et licet judici jura transgredi.* Translate this into common language, and Europeans will see one of the very many and equally senseless rules to which almost without knowing it they are subject: *In the most atrocious crimes* (that is, in the least probable) *the slightest conjectures are enough, and the judge may legitimately exceed the law.* Absurd legal practices are often the result of fear, which is the principal source of all human contradictions. Legislators (who are really only lawyers, authorised by chance to decide about everything, and to become from interested and venal writers arbiters and legislators about the fortunes of men), alarmed by the condemnation of some innocent person, have loaded jurisprudence with superfluous formalities and exceptions, the exact observance of which would cause anarchy to sit with impunity on the throne of justice. In their fright at some crimes of an atrocious nature and difficult to prove, they thought themselves under the necessity of getting over the very formalities established by themselves; and so, now with despotic impatience, now with feminine timidity, they have transformed grave trials into a kind of play, in which hazard and subterfuge act the principal part.

and modify a man's utterances, that it is almost impossible to repeat them exactly as they were spoken. Moreover, actions of a violent and unusual character, such as real crimes are, leave their traces in the numberless circumstances and effects that flow from them; and of such actions the greater the number of the circumstances adduced in proof, the more numerous are the chances for the accused to clear himself. But words only remain in the memory of their hearers, and memory is for the most part unfaithful and often deceitful. It is on that account ever so much more easy to fix a calumny upon a man's words than upon his actions.

CHAPTER IX

Secret Accusations

Palpable but consecrated abuses, which in many nations are the necessary results of a weak political constitution, are Secret Accusations. For they render men false and reserved, and whoever may suspect that he sees in his neighbour an informer will see in him an enemy. Men then come to mask their real feelings, and by the habit of hiding them from others they at last get to hide them from themselves. Unhappy they who have come to that; who, without clear and fixed principles to guide them, wander lost and confused in the vast sea of opinions, ever busied in saving themselves from the horrors that oppress them, with the present moment ever embittered by the uncertainty of the future, and without the lasting pleasures of quiet and security, devouring in unseemly haste those few pleasures, which occur at rare intervals in their melancholy lives and scarcely console them for the fact of having lived! Is it of such men we can hope to make intrepid soldiers, defenders of their country and crown? Is it among such men we shall find incorrupt magistrates, able with their free and patriotic eloquence to sustain and develop the true interests of their sovereign, ready, with the tribute they bear, to carry to the throne the love and blessings of all classes of men, and thence to bring back to palaces and cottages alike peace and security, and that active hope of ameliorating their lot which is so useful a leaven, nay, which is the life of States?

Who can protect himself from calumny, when it is armed by the strongest shield of tyranny, secrecy? What sort of government can that ever be where in every subject a ruler suspects an enemy, and is obliged for the sake of the general tranquillity to rob each individual of its possession?

What are the pretexts by which secret accusations and punishments are justified? Are they the public welfare, the security and maintenance of the form of government? But how strange a constitution is that, where he who has force on his side, and opinion, which is even stronger than force, is afraid of every citizen! Is then the indemnity of the accuser the excuse? In that case the laws do not sufficiently defend him; and shall there be subjects stronger than their sovereign? Or is it to save the informer from infamy? What! secret calumny be fair and lawful, and an open one deserving of punishment! Is it, then, the nature of the crime? If indifferent actions, or even useful actions, are called crimes, then of course accusations and trials can never be secret enough. But how can there be crimes, that is, public injuries, unless the publicity of this example, by a public trial, be at the same time the interest of all men? I respect every government, and speak of none in particular. Circumstances are sometimes such that to remove an evil may seem utter ruin when it is inherent in a national system. But had I to dictate new laws in any forgotten corner of the universe, my hand would tremble and all posterity would rise before my eyes before I would authorise such a custom as that of secret accusations.

It has already been remarked by Montesquieu that public accusations are more suited to republics, where the public good ought to be the citizens' first passion, than to monarchies, where such a sentiment is very feeble, owing to the nature of the government itself, and where the appointment of officers to accuse transgressors of the law in the name of the public is a most excellent institution. But every government, be it republican or monarchical, ought to inflict upon a false accuser the same punishment which, had the accusation been true, would have fallen upon the accused.

CHAPTER X

Suggestive Interrogations—Depositions

Our laws prohibit *suggestive* (leading) questions in a lawsuit: those, that is (according to the doctors of law), which, instead of applying, as they should do, to the *genus* in the circumstances of a crime, refer to the *species*; those, in other words, which from their immediate connection with a crime suggest to the accused a direct answer. Questions, according to the criminal lawyers, ought, so to speak, 'to envelop the main fact spirally and never to attack it in a direct line.' The reasons for this method are, either that an answer may not be *suggested* to the accused which may place him face to face with the charge against him, or perhaps because it seems unnatural for him directly to criminate himself. But, whichever of these reasons it may be, the contradiction is remarkable between the existence of such a custom and the legal authorisation of torture; for what interrogatory can be more *suggestive* than pain? The former reason applies to the question of torture, because pain will *suggest* to a strong man obstinate silence, in order that he may exchange the greater penalty for the lesser, whilst it will *suggest* to a weak man confession, in order that he may escape from present torment, which has more influence over him than pain which is to come. The other reason evidently applies too, for if a *special* question leads a man to confess against natural right, the agonies of torture will more easily do the same. But men are more governed by the difference of names than by that of things.

Finally, a man who, when examined, persists in an obstinate refusal to answer, deserves a punishment fixed by the laws, and one of the heaviest they can inflict, that men may not in this way escape the necessary example they owe to the public. But this punishment is not necessary when it is beyond all doubt that such a person has committed such a crime, questions being useless, in the same way that confession is, when other proofs sufficiently demonstrate guilt And this last case is the most usual, for experience proves that in the majority of trials the accused are wont to plead 'Not guilty.'

CHAPTER XI

Oaths

A contradiction between the laws and the natural feelings of mankind arises from the oaths which are required of an accused, to the effect that he will be a truthful man when it is his greatest interest to be false; as if a man could really swear to contribute to his own destruction, or as if religion would not be silent with most men when their interest spoke on the other side. The experience of all ages has shown that men have abused religion more than any other of the precious gifts of heaven; and for what reason should criminals respect it, when men esteemed as the wisest have often violated it? Too weak, because too far removed from the senses, are for the mass of people the motives which religion opposes to the tumult of fear and the love of life. The affairs of heaven are conducted by laws absolutely different from those which govern human affairs; so why compromise those by these? Why place men in the terrible dilemma of either sinning against God or concurring in their own ruin? The law, in fact, which enforces such an oath commands a man either to be a bad Christian or to be a martyr. The oath becomes gradually a mere formality, thus destroying the force of religious feelings, which for the majority of men are the only pledge of their honesty. How useless oaths are has been shown by experience, for every judge will bear me out when I say that no oath has ever yet made any criminal speak the truth; and the same thing is shown by reason, which declares all laws to be useless, and consequently injurious, which are opposed to the natural sentiments of man. Such laws incur the same fate as dams placed directly in the main stream of a river: either they are immediately thrown down and overwhelmed, or a whirlpool formed by themselves corrodes and undermines them imperceptibly.

CHAPTER XII

Torture

A cruelty consecrated among most nations by custom is the torture of the accused during his trial, on the pretext of compelling him to confess his crime, of clearing up contradictions in his statements, of discovering his accomplices, of purging him in some metaphysical and incomprehensible way from infamy, or finally of finding out other crimes of which he may possibly be guilty, but of which he is not accused.

A man cannot be called *guilty* before sentence has been passed on him by a judge, nor can society deprive him of its protection till it has been decided that he has broken the condition on which it was granted. What, then, is that right but one of mere might by which a judge is empowered to inflict a punishment on a citizen whilst his guilt or innocence are still undetermined? The following dilemma is no new one: either the crime is certain or uncertain; if certain, no other punishment is suitable for it than that affixed to it by law; and torture is useless, for the same reason that the criminal's confession is useless. If it is uncertain, it is wrong to torture an innocent person, such as the law adjudges him to be, whose crimes are not yet proved.

What is the political object of punishments? The intimidation of other men. But what shall we say of the secret and private tortures which the tyranny of custom exercises alike upon the guilty and the innocent? It is important, indeed, that no open crime shall pass unpunished; but the public exposure of a criminal whose crime was hidden in darkness is utterly useless. An evil that has been done and cannot be undone can only be punished by civil society in so far as it may affect others with the hope of impunity. If it be true that there are a greater number of men who either from fear or virtue respect the laws than of those who transgress them, the risk of torturing an innocent man should be estimated according to the probability that any man will have been more likely, other things being equal, to have respected than to have despised the laws.

But I say in addition: it is to seek to confound all the relations of things to require a man to be at the same time accuser and accused, to make pain the crucible of truth, as if the test of it lay in the muscles and sinews of an unfortunate wretch. The law which ordains the use of torture is a law which says to men: 'Resist pain; and if Nature has created in you an inextinguishable self-love, if she has given you an inalienable right of self-defence, I create in you a totally contrary affection, namely, an heroic self-hatred, and I command you to accuse yourselves, and to speak the truth between the laceration of your muscles and the dislocation of your bones.'

This infamous crucible of truth is a still-existing monument of that primitive and savage legal system, which called trials by fire and boiling water, or the accidental decisions of combat, *judgments of God*, as if the rings of the eternal chain in the control of the First Cause must at every moment be disarranged and put out for the petty institutions of mankind. The only difference between torture and the trial by fire and water is, that the result of the former seems to depend on the will of the accused, and that of the other two on a fact which is purely physical and extrinsic to the sufferer; but the difference is only apparent, not real. The avowal of truth under tortures and agonies is as little free as was in those times the prevention without fraud of the usual effects of fire and boiling water. Every act of our will is ever proportioned to the force of the sensible impression which causes it, and the sensibility of every man is limited. Hence the impression produced by pain may be so intense as to occupy a man's entire sensibility and leave him no other liberty than the choice of the shortest way of escape, for the present moment, from his penalty. Under such circumstances the answer of the accused is as inevitable as the impressions produced by fire and water; and the innocent man who is sensitive will declare himself guilty, when by so doing he hopes to bring his agonies to an end. All the difference between guilt and innocence is lost by virtue of the very means which they profess to employ for its discovery.

Torture is a certain method for the acquittal of robust villains and for the condemnation of innocent but feeble men. See the fatal drawbacks of this pretended test of truth—a test, indeed, that is worthy of cannibals; a test which the Romans, barbarous as they too were in many respects, reserved for slaves alone, the victims of their fierce and too highly lauded virtue. Of two men, equally innocent or equally guilty, the robust and courageous will be acquitted, the weak and the timid will be condemned, by virtue of the following exact train of reasoning on the part of the judge: 'I as judge had to find you guilty of such and such a crime; you, A B, have by your physical strength been able to resist pain, and therefore I acquit you; you, C D, in your weakness have yielded to it; therefore I condemn you. I feel that a confession extorted amid torments can have no force, but I will torture you afresh unless you corroborate what you have now confessed.'

The result, then, of torture is a matter of temperament, of calculation, which varies with each man according to his strength and sensibility; so that by this method a mathematician might solve better than a judge this problem: 'Given the muscular force and the nervous sensibility of an innocent man, to find the degree of pain which will cause him to plead guilty to a given crime.'

The object of examining an accused man is the ascertainment of truth. But if this truth is difficult to discover from a man's air, demeanour, or countenance, even when he is quiet, much more difficult will it be to discover from a man upon whose face all the signs, whereby most men, sometimes in spite of themselves, express the truth, are distorted by pain. Every violent action confuses and causes to disappear those trifling differences between objects, by which one may sometimes distinguish the true from the false.

A strange consequence that flows naturally from the use of torture is, that an innocent man is thereby placed in a worse condition than a guilty one, because if both are tortured the former has every alternative against him. For either he confesses the crime and is condemned, or he is declared innocent, having suffered an undeserved punishment. But the guilty man has one chance in his favour, since, if he resist the torture firmly, and is acquitted in consequence, he has exchanged a greater penalty for a smaller one. Therefore the innocent man can only lose, the guilty may gain, by torture.

This truth is, in fact, felt, though in a confused way, by the very persons who place themselves farthest from it. For a confession made under torture is of no avail unless it be confirmed by an oath made after it; and yet, should the criminal not confirm his confession, he is tortured afresh. Some doctors of law and some nations only allow this infamous begging of the question to be employed three times; whilst other nations and other doctors leave it to the discretion of the judge.

It were superfluous to enlighten the matter more thoroughly by mentioning the numberless instances of innocent persons who have confessed themselves guilty from the agonies of torture; no nation, no age, but can mention its own; but men neither change their natures nor draw conclusions. There is no man who has ever raised his ideas beyond the common needs of life but runs occasionally towards Nature, who with secret and confused voice calls him to herself; but custom, that tyrant of human minds, draws him back and frightens him.

The second pretext for torture is its application to supposed criminals who contradict themselves under examination, as if the fear of the punishment, the uncertainty of the sentence, the legal pageantry, the majesty of the judge, the state of ignorance that is common alike to innocent and guilty, were not enough to plunge into self-contradiction both the innocent man who is afraid, and the guilty man who seeks to shield himself; as if contradictions, common enough when men are at their ease, were not likely to be multiplied, when the mind is perturbed and wholly absorbed in the thought of seeking safety from imminent peril.

Torture, again, is employed to discover if a criminal is guilty of other crimes besides those with which he is charged. It is as if this argument were employed: 'Because you are guilty of one crime you may be guilty of a hundred others. This doubt weighs upon me: I wish to ascertain about it by my test of truth: the laws torture you because you are guilty, because you may be guilty, because I mean you to be guilty.'

Torture, again, is inflicted upon an accused man in order to discover his accomplices in crime. But if it is proved that it is not a fitting method for the discovery of truth, how will it serve to disclose accomplices, which is part of the truth to be discovered? As if a man who accuses himself would not more readily accuse others. And is it just to torment men for the crimes of others? Will not the accomplices be disclosed from the examination of the witnesses and of the accused, from the proofs and whole circumstances of the crime; in sum, from all those very means which should serve to convict the accused himself of guilt? Accomplices generally fly immediately after the capture of a companion; the uncertainty of their lot of itself condemns them to exile, and frees the country from the danger of fresh offences from them; whilst the punishment of the criminal who is caught attains its precise object, namely, the averting of other men by terror from a similar crime.

Another ridiculous reason for torture is the purgation from infamy; that is to say, a man judged infamous by the laws must confirm his testimony by the dislocation of his bones. This abuse ought not to be tolerated in the eighteenth century. It is believed that pain, which is a physical sensation, purges from infamy, which is merely a moral condition. Is pain, then, a crucible, and infamy a mixed impure substance? But infamy is a sentiment, subject neither to laws nor to reason, but to common opinion. Torture itself causes real infamy to the victim of it. So the result is, that by this method infamy will be taken away by the very fact of its infliction!

It is not difficult to go back to the origin of this ridiculous law, because the absurdities themselves that a whole nation adopts have always some connection with other common ideas which the same nation respects. The custom seems to have been derived from religious and spiritual ideas, which have so great an influence on the thoughts of men, on nations, and on generations. An infallible dogma assures us, that the stains contracted by human weakness and undeserving of the eternal anger of the Supreme Being must be purged by an incomprehensible fire. Now, infamy is a civil stain; and as pain and fire take away spiritual and incorporeal stains, why should not the agonies of torture take away the civil stain of infamy? I believe that the confession of a criminal, which some courts insist on as an essential requisite for condemnation, has a similar origin;—because in the mysterious tribunal of repentance the confession of sins is an essential part of the sacrament. This is the way men abuse the surest lights of revelation; and as these are the only ones which exist in times of ignorance, it is to them on all occasions that docile humanity turns, making of them the most absurd and far-fetched applications.

These truths were recognised by the Roman legislators, for they inflicted torture only upon slaves, who in law had no personality. They have been adopted by England, a nation, the glory of whose literature, the superiority of whose commerce and wealth, and consequently of whose power, and the examples of whose virtue and courage leave us no doubt as to the goodness of her laws. Torture has also been abolished in Sweden; it has been abolished by one of the wisest monarchs of Europe, who, taking philosophy with him to the throne, has made himself the friend and legislator of his subjects, rendering them equal and free in their dependence on the laws, the sole kind of equality and liberty that reasonable men can ask for in the present condition of things. Nor has torture been deemed necessary in the laws which regulate armies, composed though they are for the most part of the dregs of different countries, and for that reason more than any other class of men the more likely to require it. A strange thing, for whoever forgets the power of the tyranny exercised by custom, that pacific laws should be obliged to learn from minds hardened to massacre and bloodshed the most humane method of conducting trials.

CHAPTER XIII

Prosecutions and Prescriptions

As soon as the proofs of a crime and its reality are fully certified, the criminal must be allowed time and opportunity for his defence; but the time allowed must be so short as not to interfere with the speediness of his punishment, which, as we have seen, is one of the principal restraints from crime. A false philanthropy seems opposed to this shortness of time; but all doubt will vanish, on reflection that the more defective any system of law is, the greater are the dangers to which innocence is exposed.

But the laws should fix a certain space of time both for the defence of the accused and for the discovery of proofs against him. It would place the judge in the position of a legislator were it his duty to fix the time necessary for the latter. In the same way those atrocious crimes, whose memory tarries long in men's minds, deserve, when once proved, no prescription in favour of a criminal who has fled from his country; but lesser and obscure crimes should be allowed a certain prescription, which may remove a man's uncertainty concerning his fate, because the obscurity in which for a long time his crimes have been involved deducts from the bad example of his impunity, and the possibility of reform meantime remains to him. It is enough to indicate these principles, because I cannot fix a precise limit of time, except for a given system of laws and in given social circumstances. I will only add that, the advantage of moderate penalties in a nation being proved, the laws which shorten or lengthen, according to the gravity of crimes, the term of prescription or of proofs, thus making of prison itself or of voluntary exile a part of the punishment, will supply an easy classification of a few mild punishments for a very large number of crimes.

But these periods of time will not be lengthened in exact proportion to the atrocity of crimes, since the probability of a crime is in inverse ratio to its atrocity. It will, then, be necessary to shorten the period for inquiry and to increase that of prescription; which may appear to contradict what I said before, namely, that it is possible to inflict equal penalties on unequal crimes, by counting as a penalty that period of imprisonment or of prescription which precedes the verdict. To explain to the reader my idea: I distinguish two kinds of crimes—the first, atrocious crimes, beginning with homicide and including all the excessive forms of wickedness; the second comprising less considerable crimes. This distinction is founded in human nature. Personal security is a natural right, the security of property a social one. The number of motives which impel men to violate their natural affections is far smaller than those which impel them, by their natural longing for happiness, to violate a right which they do not find written in their hearts but only in the conventions of society. The very great difference between the probability of these two kinds of crime respectively makes it necessary that they should be ruled by different principles. In cases of the more atrocious crimes, because they are more uncommon, the time for inquiry ought to be so much the less as the probability of the innocence of the accused is greater; and the time of prescription ought to be longer, as on an ultimate definite sentence of guilt or innocence depends the destruction of the hope of impunity, the harm of which is proportioned to the atrocity of the crime. But in cases of lesser criminality, where the presumption in favour of a man's innocence is less, the time for inquiry should be longer; and as the harm of impunity is less, the time of prescription should be shorter. But such a division of crimes ought, indeed, not to be admitted, if the danger of impunity decreased exactly in proportion to the greater probability of the crime. One should remember that an accused man, whose guilt or innocence is uncertain, may, though acquitted for lack of proofs, be subjected for the same crime to a fresh imprisonment and inquiry, in the event of fresh legal proofs rising up against him, so long as the time of prescription accorded by the laws has not been past. Such at least is the compromise that I think best fitted to preserve both the liberty and the security of the subject, it being only too easy so to favour the one at the expense of the other, that these two blessings, the inalienable and equal patrimony of every citizen, are left unprotected and undefended, the one from declared or veiled despotism, the other from the turbulence of civil anarchy.

There are some crimes which are at the same time of common occurrence and of difficult proof. In them the difficulty of proof is equivalent to a probability of innocence; and the harm of their impunity being so much the less to be considered as their frequency depends on principles other than the risk of punishment, the time for inquiry and the period of prescription ought both to be proportionately less. Yet cases of adultery and pederasty, both of difficult proof, are precisely those in which, according to received principles, tyrannical presumptions of *quasi-proofs* and *half-proofs* are allowed to prevail (as if a man could be *half-innocent* or *half-guilty*, in other words, *half-punishable* or *half-acquittable*); in which torture exercises its cruel sway over the person of the accused, over the witnesses, and even over the whole family of an unfortunate wretch, according to the coldly wicked teaching of some doctors of law, who set themselves up as the rule and standard for judges to follow.

In view of these principles it will appear strange (to anyone who does not reflect, that reason has, so to speak, never yet legislated for a nation), that it is just the most atrocious crimes or the most secret and chimerical ones—that is, those of the least probability—which are proved by conjectures or by the weakest and most equivocal proofs: as if it were the interest of the laws and of the judge, not to search for the truth, but to find out the crime; as if the danger of condemning an innocent man were not so much the greater, the greater the probability of his innocence over that of his guilt.

The majority of mankind lack that vigour which is equally necessary for the greatest crimes as for the greatest virtues; whence it would appear, that both extremes are contemporaneous phenomena in nations which depend rather on the energy of their government and of the passions that tend to the public good, than on their size and the constant goodness of their laws. In the latter the weakened passions seem more adapted to maintain than to improve the form of government. From which flows an important consequence, namely, that great crimes in a nation do not always prove its decline.

CHAPTER XIV

Criminal Attempts, Accomplices, Impunity

It does not follow, because the laws do not punish intentions, that therefore a crime begun by some action, significative of the will to complete it, is undeserving of punishment, although it deserves less than a crime actually committed. The importance of preventing an attempt at a crime justifies a punishment; but, as there may be an interval between the attempt and the execution, the reservation of a greater punishment for a consummated crime may present a motive for its non-completion.

The same may be said, though for a different reason, where there are several accomplices of a crime, not all of them its immediate perpetrators. When several men join together in an undertaking, the greater its risk is, the more will they seek to make it equal for all of them; the more difficult it will be, therefore, to find one of them who will be willing to put the deed into execution, if he thereby incurs a greater risk than that incurred by his accomplices. The only exception would be where the perpetrator received a fixed reward, for then, the perpetrator having a compensation for his greater risk, the punishment should be equalised between him and his accomplices. Such reflections may appear too metaphysical to whosoever does not consider that it is of the utmost advantage for the laws to afford as few grounds of agreement as possible between companions in crime.

Some courts promise impunity to an accomplice in a serious crime who will expose his companions, an expedient that has its drawbacks as well as its advantages. Among the former must be counted the national authorisation of treachery, a practice which even criminals detest; for crimes of courage are less pernicious to a people than crimes of cowardice, courage being no ordinary quality, and needing only a beneficent directing force to make it conduce to the public welfare, whilst cowardice is more common and contagious, and always more self-concentrated than the other. Besides, a tribunal which calls for the aid of the law-breaker proclaims its own uncertainty and the weakness of the laws themselves. On the other hand, the advantages of the practice are, the prevention of crimes and the intimidation of the people, owing to the fact that the results are visible whilst the authors remain hidden; moreover, it helps to show that a man who breaks his faith to the laws, that is, to the public, is likely also to break it in private life. I think that a general law promising impunity to an accomplice who exposes a crime would be preferable to a special declaration in a particular case, because in this way the mutual fear which each accomplice would have of his own risk would tend to prevent their association; the tribunal would not make criminals audacious by showing that their aid was called for in a particular case. Such a law, however, should accompany impunity with the banishment of the informer.... But to no purpose do I torment myself to dissipate the remorse I feel in authorising the inviolable laws, the monument of public confidence, the basis of human morality, to resort to treachery and dissimulation. What an example to the nation it would be, were the promised impunity not observed, and were the man who had responded to the invitation of the laws dragged by learned quibbles to punishment, in spite of the public troth pledged to him! Such examples are not rare in different countries; neither, therefore, is the number small, of those who consider a nation in no other light than in that of a complicated machine, whose springs the cleverest and the strongest move at their will. Cold and insensible to all that forms the delight of tender and sensitive minds, they arouse, with imperturbable sagacity, either the softest feelings or the strongest passions, as soon as they see them of service to the object they have in view, handling men's minds just as musicians do their instruments.

CHAPTER XV

The Mildness of Punishments

From the simple consideration of the truths hitherto demonstrated it is evident that the object of punishment is neither to torment and inflict a sensitive creature nor to undo a crime already committed. Can he, whose function it is, so far from acting from passion, to tranquillise the private passions of his fellows, harbour in the body politic such useless cruelty, the instrument either of furious fanatics or of weak tyrants? Shall perchance the shrieks of an unhappy wretch call back from never-receding time actions already executed? The object, therefore, of punishment is simply to prevent the criminal from injuring anew his fellow-citizens, and to deter others from committing similar injuries; and those punishments and that method of inflicting them should be preferred which, duly proportioned to the offence, will produce a more efficacious and lasting impression on the minds of men and inflict the least torture on the body of a criminal.

Who can read history without being horror-struck at the barbarous and useless torments which men, who were called wise, in cold blood devised and executed? Who is there but must feel his blood boil, when he regards the thousands of wretches whom misery, either intended or tolerated by the laws (which have always favoured the few and outraged the many), has driven to a desperate return to the original state of nature; when he sees them either accused by men endowed with the same senses, and consequently with the same passions as themselves, of impossible crimes, the fiction of timid ignorance, or guilty of nothing but fidelity to their own principles; and when he sees them lacerated by slow tortures, subject to well-contrived formalities, an agreeable sight for a fanatical multitude?

In order that a punishment may attain its object, it is enough if the evil of the punishment exceeds the advantage of the crime, and in this excess of evil the certainty of punishment and the loss of the possible advantage from the crime ought to be considered as part; all beyond this is superfluous and consequently tyrannical. Men regulate their conduct by the reiterated impression of evils they know, not by reason of evils they ignore. Given two nations, in one of which, in the scale of punishments proportioned to the scale of crimes, the severest penalty is perpetual servitude, and in the other the wheel; I say that the former will have as great a dread of its severest punishment as the latter will have; and if there be any reason for transporting to the former country the greater penalties of the other, the same reasoning will serve for increasing still more the penalties of this latter country, passing imperceptibly from the wheel to the slowest and most elaborate tortures, nay, even to the last refinements of that science which tyrants understand only too well.

The more cruel punishments become, the more human minds harden, adjusting themselves, like fluids, to the level of objects around them; and the ever living force of the passions brings it about, that after a hundred years of cruel punishments, the wheel frightens men only just as much as at first did the punishment of prison.

The very severity of a punishment leads men to dare so much the more to escape it, according to the greatness of the evil in prospect; and many crimes are thus committed to avoid the penalty of a single one. Countries and times where punishments have been most severe have ever been those where the bloodiest and most inhuman deeds have been committed, the same spirit of ferocity that guided the hand of the legislator having guided also that of the parricide and assassin; on the throne dictating iron laws for the villanous souls of slaves to obey, and in the obscurity of private life urging to the slaughter of tyrants, only to create fresh ones in their stead.

Two other fatal consequences flow from the cruelty of punishments, and are contrary to their very purpose, the prevention of crimes. The first is, that it is not so easy to preserve the essential proportion between crime and punishment, because, however much a studied cruelty may diversify its forms, none of them can go beyond the extreme limit of endurance which is a condition of the human organisation and sensibility. When once this extreme limit is attained, it would be impossible to invent such a corresponding increase of punishment for still more injurious and atrocious crimes as would be necessary to prevent them. The other consequence is, that impunity itself arises from the severity of punishments. Men are restrained within limits both in good and evil; and a sight too atrocious for humanity can only be a passing rage, not a constant system, such as the laws ought to be; if the latter are really cruel, either they are changed, or themselves give rise to a fatal impunity.

I conclude with this reflection, that the scale of punishments should be relative to the condition of a nation. On the hardened minds of a people scarcely emerged from the savage state the impressions made should be stronger and more sensible. One needs a thunderbolt for the destruction of a fierce lion that faces round at the shot of a gun. But in proportion as men's minds become softened in the social state, their sensibility increases, and commensurate with that increase should be the diminution of the force of punishment, if it be desired to maintain any proportion between the object and the sensation that attends it.

CHAPTER XVI

Capital Punishment

This useless prodigality of punishments, by which men have never been made any better, has driven me to examine whether the punishment of death be really useful and just in a well organised government. What kind of right can that be which men claim for the slaughter of their fellow-beings? Certainly not that right which is the source of sovereignty and of laws. For these are nothing but the sum-total of the smallest portions of individual liberty, and represent the general will, that is, the aggregate of individual wills. But who ever wished to leave to other men the option of killing him? How in the least possible sacrifice of each man's liberty can there be a sacrifice of the greatest of all goods, namely, of life? And if there could be that sacrifice, how would such a principle accord with the other, that a man is not the master of his own life? Yet he must have been so, could he have given to himself or to society as a body this right of killing him.

The death penalty therefore is not a right; I have proved that it cannot be so; but it is a war of a nation against one of its members, because his annihilation is deemed necessary and expedient. But if I can show that his death is neither necessary nor expedient, I shall have won the cause of humanity.

The death of a citizen can only be deemed necessary for two reasons. The first is when, though deprived of his personal freedom, he has still such connections and power as threaten the national security; when his existence is capable of producing a dangerous revolution in the established form of government. The death of a citizen becomes then necessary when the nation is recovering or losing its liberty, or in a time of anarchy, when confusion takes the place of laws; but in times when the laws hold undisturbed sway, when the form of government corresponds with the wishes of a united nation, and is defended internally and externally by force, and by opinion which is perhaps even stronger than force, where the supreme power rests only with the real sovereign, and riches serve to purchase pleasures but not places, I see no necessity for destroying a citizen, except when his death might be the real and only restraint for diverting others from committing crimes; this latter case constituting the second reason for which one may believe capital punishment to be both just and necessary.

Since mankind generally, suspicious always of the language of reason, but ready to bow to that of authority, remain unpersuaded by the experience of all ages, in which the supreme punishment has never diverted resolute men from committing offences against society; since also they are equally unmoved by the example of the Romans and by twenty years of the reign of the Empress Elizabeth of Russia, during which she presented this illustrious example to the fathers of their people, an example which is at least equivalent to many conquests bought by the blood of her country's sons, it is sufficient merely to consult human nature itself, to perceive the truth of the assertion I have made.

The greatest effect that any punishment has upon the human mind is not to be measured by its intensity but by its duration, for our sensibility is more easily and permanently affected by very slight but repeated impressions than by a strong but brief shock. Habit holds universal sway over every sentient being, and as we speak and walk and satisfy our needs by its aid, so moral ideas only stamp themselves on our mind by long and repeated impressions. It is not the terrible yet brief sight of a criminal's death, but the long and painful example of a man deprived of his liberty, who, having become as it were a beast of burthen, repays with his toil the society he has offended, which is the strongest restraint from crimes. Far more potent than the fear of death, which men ever have before their eyes in the remote distance, is the thought, so efficacious from its constant recurrence: 'I myself shall be reduced to as long and miserable a condition if I commit similar misdeeds.'

Capital punishment makes an impression in prospect which, with all its force, does not fully meet that ready spirit of forgetfulness, so natural to man even in his most important concerns, and so liable to be accelerated by his passions. As a general rule, men are startled by the sight of violent sufferings, but not for long, and therefore such impressions are wont so to transform them as to make of ordinary men either Persians or Spartans; but in a free and settled government impressions should rather be frequent than strong.

Capital punishment becomes a spectacle for the majority of mankind, and a subject for compassion and abhorrence for others; the minds of the spectators are more filled with these feelings than with the wholesome terror the law pretends to inspire. But in moderate and continuing penalties the latter is the predominant feeling, because it is the only one. The limit, which the legislator should affix to the severity of penalties, appears to lie in the first signs of a feeling of compassion becoming uppermost in the minds of the spectators, when they look upon the punishment rather as their own than as that of the criminal.

In order that a punishment may be just, it must contain only such degrees of intensity as suffice to deter men from crimes. But as there is no one who on reflection would choose the total and perpetual loss of his liberty, however great the advantages offered him by a crime, the intensity of the punishment of servitude for life, substituted for capital punishment, has that in it which is sufficient to daunt the most determined courage. I will add that it is even more deterrent than death. Very many men face death calmly and firmly, some from fanaticism, some from vanity, which almost always attends a man to the tomb; others from a last desperate attempt either no longer to live or to escape from their misery; but neither fanaticism nor vanity have any place among fetters and chains, under the stick, under the yoke, in a cage of iron; the wretch thus punished is so far from terminating his miseries that with his punishment he only begins them.

The mind of man offers more resistance to violence and to extreme but brief pains than it does to time and to incessant weariness; for whilst it can, so to speak, gather itself together for a moment to repel the former, its vigorous elasticity is insufficient to resist the long and repeated action of the latter. In the case of capital punishment, each example presented of it is all that a single crime affords; in penal servitude for life, a single crime serves to present numerous and lasting warnings. And if it be important that the power of the laws should often be witnessed, there ought to be no long intervals between the examples of the death penalty; but this would presuppose the frequency of crimes, so that, to render the punishment effective, it must not make on men all the impression that it ought to make, in other words, it must be useful and not useful at the same time. And should it be objected that perpetual servitude is as painful as death, and therefore equally cruel, I will reply, that, taking into consideration all the unhappy moments of servitude, it will perhaps be even more painful than death; but whilst these moments are spread over the whole of a lifetime, death exercises all its force in a single moment. There is also this advantage in penal servitude, that it has more terrors for him who sees it than for him who suffers it, for the former thinks of the whole sum-total of unhappy moments, whilst the latter, by the unhappiness of the present moment, has his thoughts diverted from that which is to come. All evils are magnified in imagination, and every sufferer finds resources and consolations unknown to and unbelieved in by spectators, who substitute their own sensibility for the hardened soul of a criminal.

The following is the kind of reasoning adopted by the thief or the assassin, whose only motives for not breaking the laws are the gallows or the wheel. (I know that the analysis of one's own thoughts is an art only learnt by education, but a thief does not the less act according to certain principles because he is unable to express them). 'Of what sort,' he argues, 'are these laws that I am bound to observe, that leave so great an interval between myself and the rich man? He denies me the penny I ask of him, and excuses himself by ordering from me a work of which he himself knows nothing. Who has made these laws? Were they not made by rich and powerful men, who have never deigned to visit the wretched hovels of the poor, who have never divided a musty loaf of bread amid the innocent cries of famished children and the tears of a wife? Let us break these bonds, which are fatal to the greater number, and only useful to a few indolent tyrants; let us attack injustice in its source. I will return to my state of natural independence; I will live for some time happy and free on the fruits of my courage and address; and if the day should ever come when I have to suffer and repent for it, the time of suffering will be short, and I shall have one day of misery for many years of liberty and pleasure. As the king of a small band, I will correct the errors of fortune, and see these tyrants pale and tremble before one, whom in their insolent arrogance they rated lower than their horses or their dogs.' Then religion hovers before the mind of the criminal, who turns everything to a bad use, and offering him a facile repentance and an almost certain eternity of bliss does much to diminish in his eyes the horror of that last tragedy of all.

But the man who sees in prospect a great number of years, or perhaps the whole of his life, to be passed in servitude and suffering before the eyes of fellow-citizens with whom he is living in freedom and friendship, the slave of those laws which had once protected him, makes a useful comparison of all these circumstances with the uncertain result of his crimes and with the shortness of the time for which he would enjoy their fruits. The ever present example of those whom he actually sees the victims of their own imprudence, impresses him much more strongly than the sight of a punishment which hardens rather than corrects him.

Capital punishment is injurious by the example of barbarity it presents. If human passions, or the necessities of war, have taught men to shed one another's blood, the laws, which are intended to moderate human conduct, ought not to extend the savage example, which in the case of a legal execution is all the more baneful in that it is carried out with studied formalities. To me it seems an absurdity, that the laws, which are the expression of the public will, which abhor and which punish murder, should themselves commit one; and that, to deter citizens from private assassination, they should themselves order a public murder. What are the true and the most useful laws? Are they not those covenants and conditions which all would wish observed and proposed, when the incessant voice of private interest is hushed or is united with the interest of the public? What are every man's feelings about capital punishment? Let us read them in the gestures of indignation and scorn with which everyone looks upon the executioner, who is, after all, an innocent administrator of the public will, a good citizen contributory to the public welfare, an instrument as necessary for the internal security of a State as brave soldiers are for its external. What, then, is the source of this contradiction; and why is this feeling, in spite of reason, ineradicable in mankind? Because men in their most secret hearts, that part of them which more than any other still preserves the original form of their first nature, have ever believed that their lives lie at no one's disposal, save in that of necessity alone, which, with its iron sceptre, rules the universe.

What should men think when they see wise magistrates and grave priests of justice with calm indifference causing a criminal to be dragged by their slow procedure to death; or when they see a judge, whilst a miserable wretch in the convulsions of his last agonies is awaiting the fatal blow, pass away coldly and unfeelingly, perhaps even with a secret satisfaction in his authority, to enjoy the comforts and pleasures of life? 'Ah' they will say, 'these laws are but the pretexts of force, and the studied cruel formalities of justice are but a conventional language, used for the purpose of immolating us with greater safety, like victims destined in sacrifice to the insatiable idol of tyranny. That assassination which they preach to us as so terrible a misdeed we see nevertheless employed by them without either scruple or passion. Let us profit by the example. A violent death seemed to us a terrible thing in the descriptions of it that were made to us, but we see it is a matter of a moment. How much less terrible will it be for a man who, not expecting it, is spared all that there is of painful in it.'

Such are the fatal arguments employed, if not clearly, at least vaguely, by men disposed to crimes, among whom, as we have seen, the abuse of religion is more potent than religion itself.

If I am confronted with the example of almost all ages and almost all nations who have inflicted the punishment of death upon some crimes, I will reply, that the example avails nothing before truth, against which there is no prescription of time; and that the history of mankind conveys to us the idea of an immense sea of errors, among which a few truths, confusedly and at long intervals, float on the surface. Human sacrifices were once common to almost all nations, yet who for that reason will dare defend them? That some few states, and for a short time only, should have abstained from inflicting death, rather favours my argument than otherwise, because such a fact is in keeping with the lot of all great truths, whose duration is but as of a lightning flash in comparison with the long and darksome night that envelops mankind. That happy time has not yet arrived when truth, as error has hitherto done, shall belong to the majority of men; and from this universal law of the reign of error those truths alone have hitherto been exempt, which supreme wisdom has seen fit to distinguish from others, by making them the subject of a special revelation.

The voice of a philosopher is too feeble against the noise and cries of so many followers of blind custom, but the few wise men scattered over the face of the earth will respond to me from their inmost hearts; and, amid the many obstacles that keep it from a monarch, should truth perchance arrive in spite of him at his throne, let him know that it comes there attended by the secret wishes of all men; let him know that before his praises the bloody fame of conquerors will be silenced, and that posterity, which is just, will assign him the foremost place among the pacific triumphs of a Titus, an Antonine, or a Trajan.

Happy were humanity, if laws were now dictated to it for the first time, when we see on the thrones of Europe beneficent monarchs, men who encourage the virtues of peace, the sciences and the arts, who are fathers to their people, who are crowned citizens, and the increase of whose authority forms the happiness of their subjects, because it removes that intermediate despotism, more cruel because less secure, by which the people's wishes, always sincere, and always attended to when they can reach the throne, have been usually intercepted and suppressed. If they, I say, suffer the ancient laws to exist, it is owing to the infinite difficulties of removing from errors the revered rust of many ages; which is a reason for enlightened citizens to desire with all the greater ardour the continual increase of their authority.

CHAPTER XVII

Banishment and Confiscations

Whosoever disturbs the public peace, or obeys not the laws, that is, the conditions under which men bear with and defend one another, ought to be excluded from society, that is, to be banished from it.

Banishment, it would seem, should be employed in the case of those against whom, when accused of an atrocious crime, there is a great probability but not a certainty of guilt; but for this purpose a statute is required, as little arbitrary and as precise as possible, condemning to banishment any man who shall have placed his country in the fatal dilemma of either fearing him or of injuring him, leaving him, however, the sacred right of proving his innocence. Stronger reasons then should exist to justify the banishment of a native than of a foreigner, of a man criminated for the first time than of one who has been often so situated.

But should a man who is banished and excluded for ever from the society of which he was a member be also deprived of his property? Such a question may be regarded from different points of view. The loss of property is a greater punishment than banishment; there ought, therefore, to be some cases in which, according to his crime, a man should lose the whole, or part, or none of his property. The confiscation of the whole will occur, when the legal sentence of banishment is of a kind to annihilate all the ties that exist between society and its offending member; for in such a case the citizen dies, and only the man remains; and with regard to the political body civil death should produce the same effect as natural death. It would seem then that the confiscated property should pass to a man's lawful heirs rather than to the head of the State, since death and banishment in its extreme form are the same with regard to the body politic. But it is not by this subtlety that I dare to disapprove of confiscations of property. If some have maintained that confiscations have acted as checks on acts of revenge and on the great power of individuals, it is from neglecting to consider that, however much good punishments may effect, they are not for that reason always just, because to be just they must be necessary; and an expedient injustice can be tolerated by no legislator, who wishes to close all doors against watchful tyranny, ever ready to hold out flattering hopes, by temporary advantages and by the prosperity of a few persons of celebrity, in disregard of future ruin and of the tears of numberless persons of obscurity. Confiscations place a price on the heads of the feeble, cause the innocent to suffer the punishment of the guilty, and make the commission of crimes a desperate necessity even for the innocent. What sadder sight can there be than that of a family dragged down to infamy and misery by the crimes of its head, unable to prevent them by the submission imposed on it by the laws, even supposing such prevention to have been within its power!

CHAPTER XVIII

Infamy

Infamy is a sign of public disapprobation, depriving a criminal of the good-will of his countrymen, of their confidence, and of that feeling almost of fraternity that a common life inspires. It does not depend upon the laws. Hence the infamy which the laws inflict should be the same as that which arises from the natural relations of things, the same as that taught by universal morality, or by that particular morality, which depends on particular systems, and sets the law for ordinary opinions or for this and that nation. If the one kind of infamy is different from the other, either the law loses in public esteem, or the ideas of morality and honesty disappear, in spite of declamations, which are never efficacious against facts. Whoever declares actions to be infamous which are in themselves indifferent, detracts from the infamy of actions that are really in themselves infamous.

Corporal and painful punishments should not be inflicted for those crimes which have their foundation in pride, and draw from pain itself their glory and nutriment. For such crimes ridicule and infamy are more fitted, these being penalties which curb the pride of fanatics by the pride of the beholders, and only let truth itself escape their tenacity by slow and obstinate efforts. By such an opposition of forces against forces, and of opinions against opinions, the wise legislator destroys that admiration and astonishment among a people, which a false principle causes, whose original absurdity is usually hidden from view by the plausible conclusions deduced from it.

Penalties of infamy ought neither to be too common, nor to fall upon too many persons at a time; not too common, because the real and too frequent effects of matters of opinion weaken the force of opinion itself; not too general, because the disgrace of many persons resolves itself into the disgrace of none of them.

This, then, is the way to avoid confounding the relations and invariable nature of things, which, being unlimited by time and in ceaseless operation, confounds and overturns all narrow regulations that depart from it. It is not only the arts of taste and pleasure which have for their universal principle the faithful imitation of nature; but the art of politics itself, at least that which is true and permanent, is subject to this general maxim, since it consists in nothing else than the art of directing in the best way and to the same purposes the immutable sentiments of mankind.

CHAPTER XIX

The Promptness of Punishments

The more speedily and the more nearly in connection with the crime committed punishment shall follow, the more just and useful it will be. I say more just, because a criminal is thereby spared those useless and fierce torments of suspense which are all the greater in a person of vigorous imagination and fully conscious of his own weakness; more just also, because the privation of liberty, in itself a punishment, can only precede the sentence by the shortest possible interval compatible with the requirements of necessity. Imprisonment, therefore, is simply the safe custody of a citizen pending the verdict of his guilt; and this custody, being essentially disagreeable, ought to be as brief and easy as possible. The shortness of the time should be measured both by the necessary length of the preparations for the trial and by the seniority of claim to a judgment. The strictness of confinement should be no more than is necessary either for the prevention of escape or for guarding against the concealment of the proof of crimes. The trial itself should be finished in the shortest time possible. What contrast more cruel than that between a judge's ease and a defendant's anguish? between the comforts and pleasures of an unfeeling magistrate on the one hand, and the tears and wretchedness of a prisoner on the other? In general, the weight of a punishment and the consequence of a crime should be as efficacious as possible for the restraint of other men and as little hard as possible for the individual who is punished; for one cannot call that a proper form of society, where it is not an infallible principle, that its members intended, in constituting it, to subject themselves to as few evils as possible.

I said that the promptness of punishment is more useful, because the shorter the interval of time between the punishment and the misdeed, the stronger and the more lasting in the human mind is the association of these ideas, crime and punishment, so that insensibly they come to be considered, the one as the cause and the other as its necessary and inevitable consequence. It is a proved fact that the association of ideas is the cement of the whole fabric of the human intellect, and that without it pleasure and pain would be isolated and ineffective feelings. The further removed men are from general ideas and universal principles, that is, the more commonplace they are, the more they act by their immediate and nearest associations, to the neglect of remoter and more complex ones, the latter being of service only to men strongly impassioned for a given object of pursuit, inasmuch as the light of attention illuminates a single object, whilst it leaves the others obscure. They are also of service to minds of a higher quality, because, having acquired the habit of running rapidly over many subjects at a time, they possess facility in placing in contrast with one another many partial feelings, so that the result of their thoughts, in other words, their action, is less perilous and uncertain.

The close connection, therefore, of crime and punishment is of the utmost importance, if it be desirable that in rough and common minds there should, together with the seductive idea of an advantageous crime, immediately start up the associated idea of its punishment. Long delay has no other effect than the perpetual separation of these two ideas; and whatever the impression produced by the punishment of a crime, it produces it less as a punishment than as a sight, and only produces it when the horror of the particular crime, which would serve to strengthen the feeling of the punishment, has been weakened in the minds of the spectators.

Another principle would serve admirably to draw still closer the important connection between a misdeed and its punishment, and that is, that the latter should as far as possible conform to the nature of the crime. This analogy facilitates marvellously the contrast that ought to exist between the impulse to the crime and the counter-influence of the punishment, the one, that is, diverting the mind and guiding it to an end quite different from that to which the seductive idea of transgressing the law endeavours to lead it.

Persons guilty of lesser crimes are usually either punished in the obscurity of a prison, or transported, as an example to nations who have given no offence, to a distant and therefore almost useless servitude. Since the gravest crimes are not those which men are tempted to commit on the spur of the moment, the public punishment of a great misdeed will be regarded by most men as strange and of impossible occurrence; but the public punishment of lighter crimes, to which men's thoughts more readily incline, will make an impression, which, at the same time that it diverts the mind from them, will restrain it still more from crimes of greater gravity. Punishments should not only be proportioned to one another and to crimes in point of force, but also in the mode of their infliction.

CHAPTER XX

Certainty of Punishments—Pardons

One of the greatest preventives of crimes is, not the cruelty of the punishments attached to them, but their infallibility, and consequently that watchfulness on the part of the magistrates and that inexorable severity on the part of the judge which, to be a useful virtue, must coincide with a mild system of laws. The certainty of a punishment, moderate though it be, will ever make a stronger impression than the fear of another, more terrible, perhaps, but associated with the hope of impunity; for even the least evils when certain always terrify men's minds, and hope, that gift of heaven, which often makes up to us for everything, always throws into the distance the idea of greater evils, especially when its force is increased by impunity, which avarice and weakness so often grant.

It is sometimes the custom to release a man from the punishment of a slight crime when the injured person pardons him: an act, indeed, which is in accordance with mercy and humanity but contrary to public policy; as if a private citizen could by his remission do away with the necessity of the example in the same way that he can excuse the reparation due for the offence. The right of punishing does not rest with an individual, but with the community as a whole, or the sovereign. An individual can only renounce his particular portion of that right, not annul that of all the rest.

In proportion as punishments become milder, clemency and pardon become less necessary. Happy the nation in which their exercise should be baneful! Clemency, therefore, that virtue, which has sometimes made up in a sovereign for failings in all the other duties of the throne, ought to be excluded in a perfect system of legislation, where punishments are mild and the method of trial regular and expeditious. This truth will appear a hard one to anybody living in the present chaotic state of the criminal law, where the necessity of pardon and favours accords with the absurdity of the laws and with the severity of sentences of punishment. This right of pardon is indeed the fairest prerogative of the throne, the most desirable attribute of sovereignty; it is, however, the tacit mark of disapproval that the beneficent dispensers of the public happiness exhibit towards a code, which with all its imperfections claims in its favour the prejudice of ages, the voluminous and imposing array of innumerable commentators, the weighty apparatus of unending formalities, and the adhesion of those persons of half-learning who, though less feared than real philosophers, are really more dangerous. But let it be remembered that clemency is the virtue of the maker, not of the executor, of the laws; that it should be conspicuous in the code of laws rather than in particular judgments; that the showing to men, that crimes may be pardoned and that punishment is not their necessary consequence, encourages the hope of impunity, and creates the belief that sentences of condemnation, which might be remitted and are not, are rather violent exhibitions of force than emanations of justice. What shall be said then when the sovereign grants a pardon, that is, public immunity to an individual, and when a private act of unenlightened kindness constitutes a public decree of impunity? Let the laws therefore be inexorable and their administrators in particular cases inexorable, but let the law-maker be mild, merciful, and humane. Let him found his edifice, as a wise architect, on the basis of self-love; let the general interest be the sum of the interests of each, and he will no longer be constrained, by partial laws and violent remedies to separate at every moment the public welfare from that of individuals, and to raise the appearance of public security on fear and mistrust. As a profound and feeling philosopher let him allow men, that is, his brethren, to enjoy in peace that small share of happiness which is given them to enjoy in this corner of the universe, in that immense system established by the First Cause, by Him Who Is.

CHAPTER XXI

Asylums of Refuge

There remain two questions for me to examine: the first, whether asylums of refuge are just, and whether international agreements of extradition are expedient or not. There should be no spot within the boundaries of any country independent of the laws. Every citizen should be followed by their power, as every substance is followed by its shadow. There is only a difference of degree between impunity and the right of asylum; and as the effective influence of punishment consists more in its inevitability than in its violence, asylums do more to invite to crimes than punishments do to deter from them. The multiplication of asylums is the formation of so many petty sovereignties; for where there are no laws to command, there it is easy for new laws, opposed to the general laws of a country, to be formed, and consequently for a spirit opposed to that of the whole collective social body to arise. All history shows that from asylums have issued great revolutions in States and in the opinions of mankind.

Some persons have maintained that a crime, that is, an action contrary to the laws, is punishable wherever committed, as if the character of subject were indelible, or, in other words, synonymous with, nay, worse than, the character of slave; as if a man could be the subject of one kingdom and the resident of another, or as if his actions could without contradiction be subordinate to two sovereign powers and to two legal systems often contradictory. So some think that a cruel action done, say, at Constantinople is punishable at Paris, for the abstract reason that he who offends humanity deserves to have collective humanity for his enemy, and merits universal execration; as if judges were the avengers of human sensibility in general, and not rather of the covenants that bind men together. The place of punishment is the place of the crime, because there, and there only, is it a compulsory duty to injure an individual, to prevent an injury to the public. A villain, but one who has not broken the covenants of the society of which he was not a member, may be an object of fear, and for that reason be expelled and exiled by the superior power of that society; but he cannot be legally and formally punished, since it is for the laws to avenge, not the intrinsic malice of particular actions, but the violation of compacts.

But whether the international extradition of criminals be useful I would not venture to decide, until laws more in conformity with the needs of humanity, until milder penalties, and until the emancipation of law from the caprice of mere opinion, shall have given security to oppressed innocence and hated virtue; until tyranny shall have been confined, by the force of universal reason which ever more and more unites the interests of kings and subjects, to the vast plains of Asia; however much the conviction of finding nowhere a span of earth where real crimes were pardoned might be the most efficacious way of preventing their occurrence.

CHAPTER XXII

Of Proscription

The second question is, whether it is expedient to place a reward on the head of a known criminal, and to make of every citizen an executioner by arming him against the offender. Either the criminal has fled from his country or he is still within it. In the first case the sovereign encourages the commission of a crime and exposes its author to a punishment, being thereby guilty of an injury and of an usurpation of authority in the dominions of another, and authorising other nations to do the same by himself. In the second case the sovereign displays his own weakness, for he who has the power wherewith to defend himself seeks not to purchase it. Moreover, such an edict upsets all ideas of morality and virtue, which are ever ready to vanish from the human mind at the very slightest breath. Now the laws invite to treachery, and anon they punish it; with one hand the legislator tightens the bonds of the family, of kindred, and of friendship, whilst with the other he rewards whosoever violates and despises them; always in self-contradiction, he at one moment invites to confidence the suspicious natures of men, and at another scatters mistrust broadcast among them. Instead of preventing one crime, he causes a hundred. These are the resources of weak nations, whose laws are but the temporary repairs of a ruined building that totters throughout. In proportion as a nation becomes enlightened, good faith and mutual confidence become necessary, and tend ever more to identify themselves with true policy. Tricks, intrigues, dark and indirect paths, are for the most part foreseen, and the general quickness of all men collectively over-reaches and blunts that of single individuals. The very ages of ignorance, in which public morality inclines men to obey the dictates of private morality, serve as instruction and experience for the ages of enlightenment. But laws which reward treachery and stir up clandestine hostility by spreading mutual suspicion among citizens, are opposed to this union of private and public morality, a union which is so necessary, and to the observance of which individuals might owe their happiness, nations their peace, and the universe a somewhat longer period of quiet and repose from the evils which at present pervade it.

CHAPTER XXIII

Proportion Between Crimes and Punishments

Not only is it the general interest that crimes should not be committed, but that they should be rare in proportion to the evils they cause to society. The more opposed therefore that crimes are to the public welfare, and the more numerous the incentives to them, the stronger should be the repellent obstacles. This principle accordingly establishes the necessity of a certain proportion between crimes and punishments.

If pleasure and pain are the motors of sensitive beings, if the invisible lawgiver of humanity has decreed rewards and punishments as one of the motives to impel men to even their noblest endeavours, the inexact distribution of these motives will give rise to that contradiction, as little noticed as it is of common occurrence, namely, that the laws punish crimes which are entirely of their own creation. If an equal penalty is attached to two crimes of unequal injury to society, the greater crime of the two, if it promise a greater advantage than the other, will have no stronger motive in restraint of its perpetration. Whoever, for example, sees the same punishment of death decreed for the man who kills a pheasant and the man who slays his fellow or falsifies an important document, will draw no distinction between such crimes; and thus moral sentiments, the product only of many ages and of much bloodshed, the slowest and most difficult attainment of the human mind, dependent, it has been thought, on the aid of the most sublime motives and on a parade of the gravest formalities, will be destroyed and lost.

It is impossible to prevent all the disorders that may arise in the universal conflict of human passions. Their increase depends on that of population and on the crossings of private interests, which cannot be directed with geometrical exactness to the public welfare. In political arithmetic the calculation of probabilities must be substituted for mathematical exactness. Glance at the history of the world, and you will see disorders increase with the increase of the bounds of empire; thus national feeling being to the same extent diminished, the general inducement to crime increases with the greater interest of each individual in such disorders, and on this account the necessity for aggravating penalties ever continues to increase.

That force, similar to the force of gravitation, which constrains us to seek our own well-being, only admits of counteraction in proportion to the obstacles opposed to it. The effects of this force make up the confused series of human actions; if these clash together and impede one another, punishments, which I would call *political obstacles,* prevent bad effects from resulting, without destroying the impelling cause, which lies in the sensibility inseparable from humanity; and the legislator, in enacting them, acts the part of a clever architect, whose function it is to counteract the tendency of gravitation to cause a building to fall, and to bring to bear all the lines which contribute to its strength.

Given the necessity of the aggregation of mankind, and given the covenants which necessarily result from the very opposition of private interests, a scale of offences may be traced, beginning with those which tend directly to the destruction of society, and ending with acts of the smallest possible injustice committed against individual members of it. Between these extremes are comprised all the actions opposed to the public welfare which are called crimes, and which by imperceptible degrees decrease in enormity from the highest to the lowest. If the infinite and obscure combinations of human actions admitted of mathematical treatment, there ought to be a corresponding scale of punishments, varying from the severest to the slightest penalty. If there were an exact and universal scale of crimes and punishments, we should have an approximate and general test by which to gauge the degrees of tyranny and liberty in different governments, the relative state of the humanity or wickedness of different nations. But the wise legislator will rest satisfied with marking out the principal divisions in such a scale, so as not to invert their order, nor to affix to crimes of the first degree punishments due to those of the last.

CHAPTER XXIV

The Measure of Punishments

We have seen that the true measure of crimes is the injury done to society. This is one of those palpable truths which, however little dependent on quadrants or telescopes for their discovery, and fully within the reach of any ordinary intelligence, are yet, by a marvellous combination of circumstances, only recognised clearly and firmly by some few thinkers, belonging to every nationality and to every age. But Asiatic ideas, and passions clothed with authority and power, have, generally by imperceptible movements, sometimes by violent assaults on the timid credulity of mankind, dissipated those simple notions, which perhaps formed the first philosophy of primitive communities, and to which the enlightenment of this age seems likely to reconduct us, but to do so with that greater sureness, which can be gained from an exact investigation into things, from a thousand unhappy experiences, and from the very obstacles that militate against it.

They who have thought that the criminal's intention was the true measure of crimes were in the wrong. For the intention depends on the actual impression of things upon a man, and on his precedent mental disposition, things which vary in all men and in each man, according to the very rapid succession of his ideas, his passions, and his circumstances. It would, therefore, be necessary to form not only a particular code for each citizen, but a fresh law for every crime. Sometimes with the best intentions men do the greatest evil to society; and sometimes with the very worst they do it the greatest good.

Others again measure crimes rather by the rank of the person injured than by their importance in regard to the public weal. Were this the true measure of crimes, any act of irreverence towards the Supreme Being should be punished more severely than the assassination of a monarch, whereas the superiority of His nature affords an infinite compensation for the difference of the offence.

Lastly, some have thought that the gravity of an act's sinfulness should be an element in the measure of crimes. But an impartial observer of the true relations between man and man, and between man and God, will easily perceive the fallacy of this opinion. For the former relationship is one of equality; necessity alone, from the clash of passions and opposing interests, having given rise to the idea of the *public utility*, the basis of human justice. But the other relationship is one of dependence on a perfect Being and Creator, who has reserved to Himself alone the right of being at the same time legislator and judge, and can alone unite the two functions without bad effects. If He has decreed eternal punishments to those who disobey His omnipotence, what insect shall dare to take the place of Divine justice, or shall wish to avenge that Being, who is all-sufficient to Himself, who can receive from things no impression of pleasure nor of pain, and who alone of all beings acts without reaction? The degree of sinfulness in an action depends on the unsearchable wickedness of the heart, which cannot be known by finite beings without a revelation. How, then, found thereon a standard for the punishment of crimes? In such a case men might punish when God pardons, and pardon when God punishes. If men can act contrary to the Almighty by offending Him, they may also do so in the punishments they inflict.

CHAPTER XXV

The Division of Punishments

Some crimes tend directly to the destruction of society or to the sovereign who represents it; others affect individual citizens, by imperilling their life, their property, or their honour; whilst others, again, are actions contrary to the positive or negative obligations which bind every individual to the public weal.

Any action that is not included between the two above-indicated extremes can only be called a *crime* or punished as such by those who find their interest in so calling it. The uncertainty of these limits has produced in different nations a system of ethics contrary to the system of laws, has produced many actual systems of laws at total variance with one another, and a quantity of laws which expose even the wisest man to the severest penalties. Consequently the words *virtue* and *vice* have become of vague and variable meaning, and from the uncertainty thus surrounding individual existence, listlessness and a fatal apathy have spread over political communities.

The opinion that each citizen should have liberty to do whatsoever is not contrary to the laws, without fear of any other inconvenience than such as may arise from the action itself—this is the political dogma that should be believed by the people and promulgated by the chief magistrates, a dogma as sacred as that of the incorrupt guardianship of the laws, without which there can be no legitimate society; a just compensation to mankind for their sacrifice of that entire liberty of action which belongs to every sensitive being, and is only limited by the extent of its force. This it is that forms liberal and vigorous souls, and enlightened minds; that makes men virtuous with that virtue which can resist fear, and not with that flexible kind of prudence which is only worthy of a man who can put up with a precarious and uncertain existence.

Whosoever will read with a philosophical eye the codes and annals of different nations will find almost always that the names of *virtue* and *vice*, of *good citizen* and *criminal*, are changed in the course of ages, not in accordance with the changes that occur in the circumstances of a country, and consequently in conformity with the general interest, but in accordance with the passions and errors that have swayed different legislators in succession. He will observe full often, that the passions of one age form the basis of the morality of later ones; that strong passions, the offspring of fanaticism and enthusiasm, weakened and, so to speak, gnawed away by time (which reduces to a level all physical and moral phenomena) become little by little the prudence of the age, and a useful instrument in the hand of the strong man and the clever. In this way the vaguest notions of honour and virtue have been produced; for they change with the changes of time, which causes names to survive things; as also with the changes of rivers and mountains, which form frequently the boundaries of moral no less than of physical geography.

CHAPTER XXVI

Crimes of High Treason

The first class of crimes—that is, the worst, because they are the most injurious to society—are those known as crimes of high treason. Only tyranny and ignorance, which confound words and ideas of the clearest meaning, can apply this name, and consequently the heaviest punishment, to different kinds of crimes, thus rendering men, as in a thousand other cases, the victims of a word. Every crime, be it ever so private, injures society; but every crime does not aim at its immediate destruction. Moral, like physical actions, have their limited sphere of activity, and are differently circumscribed, like all the movements of nature, by time and space; and therefore only a sophistical interpretation, which is generally the philosophy of slavery, can confound what eternal truth has distinguished by immutable differences.

CHAPTER XXVII

Crimes Against Personal Security—Acts of Violence—Punishments of Nobles

After crimes of high treason come crimes opposed to the personal security of individuals. This security being the primary end of every properly constituted society, it is impossible not to affix to the violation of any citizen's right of personal security one of the severest punishments that the laws allow.

Some crimes are injuries to a man's person, others to his property, and the former should certainly be punished by corporal punishments.

Offences, therefore, against personal security and liberty are among the greatest of crimes. Under this head fall not only the assassinations and thefts of the common people, but those also committed by the nobles and magistrates, whose influence, acting with greater force and to a greater distance, destroys in those subject to them all ideas of justice and duty, and gives strength to those ideas of the right of the strongest, which are equally perilous ultimately to him who exercises no less than to him who endures it.

Neither the noble nor the rich man ought to be able to pay a price for injuries committed against the feeble and the poor; else riches, which, under the protection of the laws, are the prize of industry, become the nourishment of tyranny. Whenever the laws suffer a man in certain cases to cease to be a *person* and to become a *thing*, there is no liberty; for then you will see the man of power devoting all his industry to gather from the numberless combinations of civil life those which the law grants in his favour. This discovery is the magic secret that changes citizens into beasts of burden, and in the hand of the strong man forms the chain wherewith to fetter the actions of the imprudent and the weak. This is the reason why in some governments, that have all the semblance of liberty, tyranny lies hidden or insinuates itself unforeseen, in some corner neglected by the legislator, where insensibly it gains force and grows.

Men oppose the strongest barriers against open tyranny, but they see not the imperceptible insect, which gnaws them away, and makes for the invading stream an opening that is all the more sure by very reason of its concealment from view.

Of what kind, then, will be the punishments due to the crimes of nobles, whose privileges form so great a part of the laws of different countries? I will not here inquire whether this traditional distinction between nobles and commons be advantageous in a government, or necessary in a monarchy; nor whether it be true that a nobility forms an intermediate power in restraint of the excesses of the two extremes, and not rather a caste which, in slavery to itself and to others, confines all circulation of merit and hope to a very narrow circle, like those fertile and pleasant oases scattered among the vast sand-deserts of Arabia; nor whether, supposing it to be true that inequality is inevitable and useful in society, it be also true that such inequality should subsist between classes rather than individuals, and should remain with one part of the body politic rather than circulate through the whole; whether it should rather perpetuate itself than be subject to constant self-destruction and renovation. I will confine myself to the punishments proper for nobles, affirming that they should be the same for the greatest citizen as for the least. Every distinction of honour or of riches presupposes, to be legitimate, a prior state of equality, founded on the laws, which regard all subjects as equally dependent on themselves. One must suppose the men, who renounced their natural state of despotic independence, to have said: 'Let him who is more industrious than his fellows have greater honours, and let his fame be greater among his successors; let him who is more prosperous and honoured hope even to become more so, but let him fear no less than other men to break those conditions by virtue of which he is raised above them.' True it is that such decrees did not emanate in a convocation of the human race, but such decrees exist in the eternal relations of things; they do not destroy the supposed advantages of a nobility, though they prevent its abuses; and they make laws feared, by closing every admission to impunity. And if any one shall say that the same punishment inflicted upon a noble and upon a commoner is not really the same, by reason of the diversity of their education, and of the disgrace spread over an illustrious family, I will reply, that the sensibility of the criminal is not the measure of punishment, but the public injury, and that this is all the greater when committed by the more highly favoured man; that equality of punishment can only be so when considered extrinsically, being really different in each individual; and that the disgrace of a family can be removed by public proofs of kindness on the part of the sovereign towards the innocent family of the criminal. And who is there but knows that formalities which strike the senses serve as reasonings with the credulous and admiring populace?

CHAPTER XXVIII

Of Injuries and of Honour

Injuries that are personal and affect a man's honour—that is, the fair share of favour that he has a right to expect from others—should be punished with disgrace.

There is a remarkable contradiction between the civil laws, which set so jealous and supreme a guard upon individual life and property, and the laws of so-called *honour*, which set opinion above everything. This word *honour* is one of those that have served as the basis for long and brilliant argumentations, without any fixed or permanent idea being attached to it. How miserable is the condition of human minds, more distinctly cognisant of the remotest and least important ideas about the movements of the heavenly bodies, than of those near and important moral notions, which are ever fluctuating and confused, according as the winds of passion impel them and a well-guided ignorance receives and transmits them! But the seeming paradox will vanish, if one considers, that, as objects become confused when too near the eyes, so the too great propinquity of moral ideas easily causes the numerous simple ideas which compose them to become blended together, to the confusion of those clear lines of demarcation demanded by the geometrical spirit, which would fain measure exactly the phenomena of human sensibility. And the wonder will vanish altogether from the impartial student of human affairs, who will suspect that so great a moral machinery and so many restraints are perchance not needed, in order to render men happy and secure.

This *honour*, then, is one of those complex ideas which are an aggregate not only of simple ideas but of ideas no less complex than themselves, and which in their various presentments to the mind now admit and now omit some of their different component elements, only retaining some few common ideas, just as in algebra several complex quantities admit of a common divisor. To find this common divisor in the different ideas that men form of *honour*, we must cast a rapid glance over the first formation of communities.

The necessity of remedying the disorders caused by the physical despotism of each man singly produced the first laws and the first magistrates; this was the end and object of the institution of societies, and this end has always been maintained, either in reality or appearance, at the head of all codes, even of those that operated otherwise. But the closer contact of men with one another and the progress of their knowledge brought about an endless series of mutual actions and needs, which ever lay beyond the foresight of the laws and below the actual power of individuals. From this epoch began the despotism of opinion, which afforded the only means for obtaining from others those benefits and averting those evils, for which the laws failed to provide. It is this opinion that is the trouble equally of the wise man and the fool; that has raised the semblance of virtue to higher credit than virtue itself; that even makes the rascal turn missionary, because he finds his own interest therein. Hence the favour of men became not only useful but necessary, if a man would not fall below the general level. Hence, not only does the ambitious man seek after such favour as useful to himself, and the vain man go begging for it as a proof of his merit, but the man of honour also may be seen to require it as a necessity. This *honour* is a condition that very many men attach to their own existence. Born after the formation of society, it could not be placed in the general deposit; it is rather a momentary return to the state of nature, a momentary withdrawal of one's self from the dominion of those laws which, under the circumstances, fail to afford the sufficient defence required of them.

Hence both in the state of extreme political liberty and in that of extreme political subjection the ideas of honour disappear or get perfectly confused with others. For in the former the despotism of the laws renders the pursuit of the favour of others of no avail; and in the latter state the despotism of men, by destroying civil existence, reduces everybody to a precarious and temporary personality. Honour, therefore, is one of the fundamental principles of those monarchies that are a mitigated form of despotism, being to them what revolutions are to despotic States, namely, a momentary return to the state of nature, and a reminder to the chief ruler of the condition of primitive equality.

CHAPTER XXIX

Duels

From this necessity of the favour of other people arose private duels, which sprang up precisely in an anarchical state of the laws. It is said they were unknown to antiquity, perhaps because the ancients did not meet suspiciously armed in the temples, the theatres, or with friends; perhaps because the duel was an ordinary and common sight, presented to the people by gladiators, who were slaves or low people, and freemen disdained to be thought and called private gladiators. In vain has it been sought to extirpate the custom by edicts of death against any man accepting a challenge, for it is founded on that which some men fear more than death; since without the favour of his fellows the man of honour foresees himself exposed either to become a merely solitary being, a condition insufferable to a sociable man, or to become the butt of insults and disgrace which, from their constant operation, prevail over the fear of punishment. Why is it that the lower orders do not for the most part fight duels like the great? Not only because they are disarmed, but because the need of the favour of others is less general among the people than among those who, in higher ranks, regard themselves with greater suspicion and jealousy.

It is not useless to repeat what others have written, namely, that the best method of preventing this crime is to punish the aggressor—in other words, the man who gives rise to the duel—declaring him to be innocent who without his own fault has been constrained to defend that which existing laws do not assure to him, that is, opinion.

CHAPTER XXX

Thefts

Thefts without violence should be punished by fine. He who enriches himself at another's expense ought to suffer at his own. But, as theft is generally only the crime of wretchedness and despair, the crime of that unhappy portion of mankind to whom the right of property (a terrible, and perhaps not necessary right[67]) has left but a bare subsistence; and as pecuniary penalties increase the number of criminals above the number of crimes, depriving the innocent of their bread in order to give it to the wicked, the fittest punishment will be that kind of servitude which alone can be called just, namely, the temporary servitude of a man's labour and person for the compensation of society, the personal and absolute dependence due from a man who has essayed to exercise an unjust superiority over the social compact. But when the theft is accompanied with violence, the punishment also should be a combination of corporal and servile punishment. Some previous writers have shown the evident abuse that arises from not distinguishing punishments for thefts of violence from those for thefts of cunning, thus making an absurd equation between a large sum of money and the life of a man. For they are crimes of a different nature; and in politics, as in mathematics, this axiom is most certain, that between heterogeneous quantities the terms of difference are infinite; but it is never superfluous to repeat what has hardly ever been put into practice. Political machinery more than anything else retains the motion originally given to it, and is the slowest to adapt itself to a fresh one.

67 In the original manuscript and the first edition there was no *not*. It is unknown how it got in, or whether Beccaria was aware of it. Cantù, *Beccaria*, 127.

CHAPTER XXXI

Smuggling

Smuggling is a real crime against the sovereign and the nation; but its punishment should not be one of disgrace, because its commission incurs no disgrace in public opinion.

But why does this crime never entail disgrace upon its author, seeing that it is a theft against the prince, and consequently against the nation? I answer, that offences which men do not consider can be committed against themselves do not interest them enough to produce public indignation against their perpetrator. Smuggling is an offence of this character. Men in general, on whom remote consequences make very feeble impressions, do not perceive the harm that smuggling can do them, nay, often they enjoy a present advantage from it. They only perceive the injury done to the sovereign; they are not interested, therefore, in withdrawing their favour from a smuggler as much as they are in doing so from a man who commits a theft in private life, who forges a signature, or brings upon them other evils. The principle is self-evident, that every sensitive being only interests himself in the evils which he knows. This crime arises from the law itself; since the benefit it promises increases with the increase of the import duty, and therefore the temptation and the facility of committing it increases with the circumference of territory to be guarded and the small size of the prohibited wares. The penalty of losing both the prohibited goods, and whatever effects are found with them, is most just; but its efficacy will be greater in proportion as the import duty is lower, because men only incur risks relative to the advantage derivable from the prosperous issue of their undertaking.

But ought such a crime to be let go unpunished in the case of a man who has no effects to lose? No: there are kinds of smuggling of so much importance to the revenue (which is so essential and so difficult a part of a good system of laws), that such a crime deserves a considerable punishment, even imprisonment or servitude; but imprisonment and servitude conformable to the nature of the crime itself. For example, the prison of the tobacco-smuggler ought not to be the same as that of the assassin or the thief; and the labours of the former, limited to the work and service of the very treasury he wished to defraud, will be the punishments most conformable to the nature of his crime.

CHAPTER XXXII

Of Debtors

The good faith of contracts and the security of commerce compel the legislator to assure to creditors the persons of insolvent debtors. But I think it important to distinguish the fraudulent from the innocent bankrupt, the former of whom should receive the same punishment as that assigned to false coiners, since it is no greater crime to falsify a piece of coined money, the pledge of men's mutual obligations, than to falsify those obligations themselves. But the innocent bankrupt—he who, after a searching inquiry, has proved before his judges that the wickedness or misfortune of some one else, or the inevitable vicissitudes of human prudence, have despoiled him of his substance—for what barbarous reason ought such an one to be thrown into prison, and deprived of the only poor benefit that remains to him, a barren liberty, in order to suffer the agonies of the really guilty, and, in despair at his ruined honesty, to repent perhaps of that innocence, by which he lived peacefully under the protection of those laws that it was not in his power not to offend against? Laws, too, dictated by the powerful by reason of their rapacity, and endured by the feeble by reason of that hope, which generally glimmers in the human heart, and leads us to believe that unfavourable contingencies are reserved for others, favourable ones for ourselves! Men left to their natural feelings love cruel laws, however much, as subject to them themselves, it might be for their individual interest that they should be mitigated; because their fear of being injured by others is greater than their desire to inflict injuries themselves.

To return to the innocent bankrupt. Granting that his obligation should not be extinguishable by anything short of total payment; granting that he should not be suffered to withdraw from it without the consent of the parties interested, nor to transfer under the dominion of other laws his industry, which should perforce be employed, under penalties, to enable him to satisfy his creditors in proportion to his profits; what fair pretext, I ask, can there be, such as the security of commerce or the sacred right of property, to justify the deprivation of his liberty? Such a deprivation is only of use, when it is sought to discover the secrets of a supposed innocent bankrupt by the evils of servitude, a most unusual circumstance where a rigorous inquiry is instituted. I believe it to be a maxim in legislation, that the amount of political inconveniences varies directly in proportion to the injury they do the public, and inversely in proportion to the difficulty of their proof.

It would be possible to distinguish a case of fraud from a grave fault, a grave fault from a light one, and this again from perfect innocence; then to affix to the first the penalties due for crimes of falsification; to the second lesser penalties, but with the loss of personal liberty; and, reserving for the last degree the free choice of the means of recovery, to deprive the third degree of such liberty, whilst leaving it to a man's creditors. But the distinction between grave and light should be fixed by the blind impartiality of the laws, not by the dangerous and arbitrary wisdom of a judge. The fixings of limits are as necessary in politics as in mathematics, equally in the measurement of the public welfare as in the measurement of magnitudes.[68]

How easily might the farseeing legislator hinder a large part of culpable bankruptcy, and relieve the misfortunes of the industrious and innocent! The public and open registration of all contracts; freedom to every citizen to consult them in well-kept documents; a public bank formed by wisely-apportioned taxes upon prosperous commerce, and intended for the timely relief of any unfortunate and innocent member of the company;—such measures would have no real drawback and might produce numberless advantages. But easy, simple, and great laws, which await but the signal of the legislator, in order to scatter riches and strength through a nation—laws which would be celebrated from generation to generation in hymns of gratitude—are either the least thought of or the least desired of all. An uneasy and petty spirit, the timid prudence of the present moment, and a circumspect stiffness against innovations, master the feelings of those who govern the complex actions of mankind.

---

68 Commerce and property are not themselves an end of the social compact, but they may be a means to reach that end. To expose all the members of society to evils, for the production of which so many circumstances work together, would be to subordinate ends to means—a paralogism of all the sciences, but especially of political science, and one into which I fell in the first editions, where I said that the innocent bankrupt ought to be kept guarded in pledge of his debts or employed as a slave to labour for his creditors. I am ashamed of having so written. I have been accused of irreligion without deserving to be, and I have been accused of sedition without deserving to be. I offended the rights of humanity, and no one reproached me for it!

CHAPTER XXXIII

Of The Public Tranquillity

Lastly, among the crimes of the third kind are especially those which disturb the public peace and civic tranquillity; such as noises and riots in the public streets, which were made for the convenience of men and traffic, or fanatical sermons that excite the easily roused passions of the curious multitude. For their passions gather force from the number of hearers, and more from a certain obscure and mysterious enthusiasm, than from clear and quiet reasoning, which never has any influence over a large mass of men.

The lighting of a city by night at the public expense; the distribution of guards in the different quarters; simple moral discourses on religion, but only in the silent and holy quiet of churches, protected by public authority; speeches on behalf of private and public interests in national assemblies, parliaments, or wherever else the majesty of sovereignty resides—all these are efficacious means for preventing the dangerous condensation of popular passions. These means are a principal branch of that magisterial vigilance which the French call *police*; but if this is exercised by arbitrary laws, not laid down in a code of general circulation, a door is opened to tyranny, which ever surrounds all the boundaries of political liberty. I find no exception to this general axiom, that 'Every citizen ought to know when his actions are guilty or innocent.' If censors, and arbitrary magistrates in general, are necessary in any government, it is due to the weakness of its constitution, and is foreign to the nature of a well organised government. More victims have been sacrificed to obscure tyranny by the uncertainty of their lot than by public and formal cruelty, for the latter revolts men's minds more than it abases them. The true tyrant always begins by mastering opinion, the precursor of courage; for the latter can only show itself in the clear light of truth, in the fire of passion, or in ignorance of danger.

CHAPTER XXXIV

Of Political Idleness

Wise governments suffer not political idleness in the midst of work and industry. I mean by political idleness that existence which contributes nothing to society either by its work or by its wealth; which gains without ever losing; which, stupidly admired and reverenced by the vulgar, is regarded by the wise man with disdain, and with pity for the beings who are its victims; which, being destitute of that stimulus of an active life, the necessity of preserving or increasing the store of worldly goods, leaves to the passions of opinion, not the least strong ones, all their energy. This kind of idleness has been confused by austere declaimers with that of riches, gathered by industry; but it is not for the severe and narrow virtue of some censors, but for the laws, to define what is punishable idleness. He is not guilty of political idleness, who enjoys the fruits of the virtues or vices of his ancestors and sells in exchange for his pleasures bread and existence to the industrious poor, who carry on peacefully the silent war of industry against wealth, instead of by force a war uncertain and sanguinary. The latter kind of idleness is necessary and useful, in proportion as society becomes wider and its government more strict.

CHAPTER XXXV

Suicide and Absence

Suicide is a crime to which a punishment properly so called seems inadmissible, since it can only fall upon the innocent or else upon a cold and insensible body. If the latter mode of punishing the crime makes no more impression on the living than would be made by inflicting violence on a statue, the other mode is unjust and tyrannical, inasmuch as political freedom necessarily presupposes the purely personal nature of punishment. Men love life only too much, and everything that surrounds them confirms them in this love. The seductive image of pleasure, and hope, that sweetest illusion of mortals, for the sake of which they swallow large draughts of evil mixed with a few drops of contentment, are too attractive, for one ever to fear, that the necessary impunity of such a crime should exercise any general influence. He who fears pain, obeys the laws; but death puts an end in the body to all the sources of pain. What, then, will be the motive which shall restrain the desperate hand of the suicide?

Whoever kills himself does a lesser evil to society than he who for ever leaves the boundaries of his country, for whilst the former leaves therein all his substance, the latter transports himself together with part of his property. Nay, if the power of a community consists in the number of its members, the man who withdraws himself to join a neighbouring nation does twice as great an injury as he who simply by death deprives society of his existence. The question, therefore, reduces itself to this: whether the leaving to each member of a nation a perpetual liberty to absent himself from it be advantageous or detrimental.

No law ought to be promulgated that has not force to back it, or that the nature of things deprives of validity; and as minds are ruled by opinion, which itself follows the slow and indirect impressions of legislation, whilst it resists those that are direct and violent, the most salutary laws become infected with the contempt felt for useless laws, and are regarded rather as obstacles to be surmounted than as the deposit of the public welfare.

Moreover, if, as was said, our feelings are limited in quantity, the greater respect men may have for things outside the laws, the less will remain to them for the laws themselves. From this principle the wise administrator of the public happiness may draw some useful consequences, the exposition of which would lead me too far from my subject, which is to demonstrate the uselessness of making a prison of the State. A law with such an object is useless, because, unless inaccessible rocks or an unnavigable sea separate a country from all others, how will it be possible to close all the points of its circumference and keep guard over the guardians themselves? A man who transports everything he has with him, when he has done so cannot be punished. Such a crime once committed can no longer be punished, and to punish it beforehand would be to punish men's wills, not their actions, to exercise command over their intention, the freest part of human nature, and altogether independent of the control of human laws. The punishment of an absent man in the property he leaves behind him would ruin all international commerce, to say nothing of the facility of collusion, which would be unavoidable, except by a tyrannical control of contracts. And his punishment on his return, as a criminal, would prevent the reparation of the evil done to society, by making all removals perpetual. The very prohibition to leave a country augments people's desire to do so, and is a warning to foreigners not to enter it.

What should we think of a government that has no other means than fear for keeping men in a country, to which they are naturally attached from the earliest impressions of their infancy? The surest way of keeping them in their country is to augment the relative welfare of each of them. As every effort should be employed to turn the balance of commerce in our own favour, so it is the greatest interest of a sovereign and a nation, that the sum of happiness, compared with that of neighbouring nations, should be greater at home than elsewhere. The pleasures of luxury are not the principal elements in this happiness, however much they may be a necessary remedy to that inequality which increases with a country's progress, and a check upon the tendency of wealth to accumulate in the hands of a single ruler.[69]

---

69 Where a country's boundaries increase at a greater rate than its population, there luxury favours despotism, firstly, because scarcity of men means less industry, and less industry means a greater dependence of poverty upon wealth, and greater difficulty and less dread of a combination of the oppressed against their oppressors; secondly, because the flatteries, the services, the distinctions, the submission, which cause the difference between the strong man and the feeble to be all the more felt, are

But commerce and the interchange of the pleasures of luxury have this drawback, that however many persons are engaged in their production, they yet begin and end with a few, the great majority of men only enjoying the smallest share of them, so that the feeling of misery, which depends more on comparison than on reality, is not prevented. But the principal basis of this happiness I speak of is personal security and liberty under the limitations of the law; with these the pleasures of luxury favour population, and without them they become the instrument of tyranny. As the noblest wild beasts and the freest birds remove to solitudes and inaccessible forests, leaving the fertile and smiling plains to the wiles of man, so men fly from pleasures themselves when tyranny acts as their distributor.

It is, then, proved that the law which imprisons subjects in their own country is useless and unjust. The punishment, therefore, of suicide is equally so; and consequently, although it is a fault punishable by God, for He alone can punish after death, it is not a crime in the eyes of men, for the punishment they inflict, instead of falling on the criminal himself, falls on his family. If anyone objects, that such a punishment can nevertheless draw a man back from his determination to kill himself, I reply, that he who calmly renounces the advantages of life, who hates his existence here below to such an extent as to prefer to it an eternity of misery, is not likely to be moved by the less efficacious and more remote consideration of his children or his relations.

---

more easily obtained from few men than from many, since men are more independent the less subject they are to observation, and are the less subject to observation the more numerous they are. But where the population increases at a faster rate than the boundaries are enlarged, luxury is opposed to despotism, because it gives life to men's industry and activity, and the necessity of the poor man offers too many pleasures and comforts to the rich man for the pleasures of pure ostentation, which increase the idea of dependence, to have the greater place. Hence it is observable that in large, weak, and depopulated States, unless there are counteracting causes, the luxury of ostentation prevails over the luxury of comfort; but in populous rather than large States the luxury of comfort always causes the diminution of that of ostentation.

CHAPTER XXXVI

Crimes of Difficult Proof

There are some crimes which, are at the same time frequent in society and yet difficult to prove, as adultery, pederasty, infanticide.

Adultery is a crime which, politically considered, derives its force and direction from two causes, namely, from the variable laws in force among mankind, and from that strongest of all attractions which draws one sex towards the other.[70]

Had I to address nations still destitute of the light of religion, I would say that there is yet another considerable difference between adultery and other crimes. For it springs from the abuse of a constant and universal human impulse, an impulse anterior to, nay, the cause of the institution of society; whereas other crimes, destructive of society, derive their origin rather from momentary passions than from a natural impulse. To anyone cognisant of history and his kind, such an impulse will seem to be equivalent in the same climate to a constant quantity; and if this be so, those laws and customs which seek to diminish the sum-total will be useless or dangerous, because their effect will be to burthen one half of humanity with its own needs and those of others; but those laws, on the contrary, will be the wisest, which following, so to speak, the gentle inclination of the plain, divide the total amount, causing it to ramify into so many equal and small portions, that aridity or overflowing are equally prevented everywhere. Conjugal fidelity is always proportioned to the number and to the freedom of marriages. Where marriages are governed by hereditary prejudices, or bound or loosened by parental power, there the chains are broken by secret intrigue, in despite of ordinary morality, which, whilst conniving at the causes of the offence, makes it its duty to declaim against the results. But there is no need of such reflections for the man who, living in the light of true religion, has higher motives to correct

70 This attraction resembles in many points that of gravitation, which moves the universe, because, like it, it diminishes with distance; and if the one force controls all the movements of physical bodies, the other controls those of the mind during the continuance of its sway. But they differ in this, that, whilst gravitation is counterbalanced by obstacles, the other for the most part gains force and strength from the increase of the very obstacles opposed to it.

the force of natural effects. Such a crime is of so instantaneous and secret commission, so concealed by the very veil the laws have drawn round it (a veil necessary, indeed, but fragile, and one that enhances, instead of diminishing, the value of the desired object), the occasions for it are so easy, and the consequences so doubtful, that the legislator has it more in his power to prevent than to punish it. As a general rule, in every crime which by its nature must most frequently go unpunished, the penalty attached to it becomes an incentive. It is a quality of our imagination, that difficulties, if they are not insurmountable nor too difficult, relatively to the mental energy of the particular person, excite the imagination more vividly, and place the object desired in larger perspective; for they serve as it were as so many barriers to prevent an erratic and flighty fancy from quitting hold of its object; and, while they compel the imagination to consider the latter in all its bearings, it attaches itself more closely to the pleasant side, to which our mind most naturally inclines, than to the painful side, which it places at a distance.

Pederasty, so severely punished by the laws, and so readily subjected to the tortures that triumph over innocence, is founded less on the necessities of man, when living in a state of isolation and freedom, than on his passions when living in a state of society and slavery. It derives its force not so much from satiety of pleasure as from the system of education now in vogue, which, beginning by making men useless to themselves in order to make them useful to others, causes, by its too strict seclusion, a waste of all vigorous development, and accelerates the approach of old age.

Infanticide equally is the result of the unavoidable dilemma in which a woman is placed who from weakness or by violence has fallen. Finding herself placed between the alternative of infamy on the one side, and the death of a being insentient of its pains on the other, how can she fail to prefer the latter to the infallible misery awaiting both herself and her unhappy offspring? The best way to prevent this crime would be to give efficient legal protection to weakness against tyranny, which exaggerates those vices that cannot be hidden by the cloak of virtue.

I do not pretend to diminish the just wrath these crimes deserve; but, in indicating their sources, I think myself justified in drawing one general conclusion, and that is, that no punishment for a crime can be called exactly just—that is, necessary—so long as the law has not adopted the best possible means, in the circumstances of a country, to prevent the crimes it punishes.

CHAPTER XXXVII

Of a Particular Kind of Crime

The reader of this treatise will perceive that I have omitted all reference to a certain class of crime, which has deluged Europe with human blood; a crime which raised those fatal piles, where living human bodies served as food for the flames, and where the blind multitude sought a pleasant spectacle and a sweet harmony from the low dull groans, emitted by wretched sufferers from volumes of black smoke, the smoke of human limbs, whilst their bones and still palpitating entrails were scorched and consumed by the flames. But reasonable men will see that the place, the age, and the subject suffer me not to inquire into the nature of such a crime. It would be too long and remote from my subject to show, how a perfect uniformity of thought ought, contrary to the practice of many countries, to be a necessity in a State; how opinions, which only differ by the most subtle and imperceptible degrees, and are altogether beyond the reach of human intelligence, can yet convulse society, when one of them is not legally authorised in preference to the others; and how the nature of opinions is such, that, whilst some become clearer by virtue of their conflict and opposition, (those that are true floating and surviving, but those that are false sinking to oblivion,) others again, with no inherent self-support, require to be clothed with authority and power. Too long would it be to prove, that howsoever hateful may seem the government of force over human minds, with no other triumphs to boast of but dissimulation and debasement, and howsoever contrary it may seem to the spirit of gentleness and fraternity, commanded alike by reason and the authority we most venerate, it is yet necessary and indispensable. All this should be taken as clearly proved and conformable to the true interests of humanity, if there be anyone who, with recognised authority, acts accordingly. I speak only of crimes that spring from the nature of humanity and the social compact; not of sins, of which even the temporal punishments should be regulated by other principles than those of a narrow philosophy.

CHAPTER XXXVIII

False Ideas of Utility

False ideas of utility entertained by legislators are one source of errors and injustice. It is a false idea of utility which thinks more of the inconvenience of individuals than of the general inconvenience; which tyrannises over men's feelings, instead of arousing them into action; which says to Reason, 'Be thou subject.' It is a false idea of utility which sacrifices a thousand real advantages for one imaginary or trifling drawback; which would deprive men of the use of fire because it burns or of water because it drowns; and whose only remedy for evils is the entire destruction of their causes. Of such a kind are laws prohibiting the wearing of arms, for they only disarm those who are not inclined nor resolved to commit crimes, whilst those who have the courage to violate the most sacred laws of humanity, the most important in the law-code, are little likely to be induced to respect those lesser and purely arbitrary laws, which are easier to contravene with impunity; and the strict observance of which would imply the destruction of all personal liberty, (that liberty dearest to the enlightened legislator and to men generally,) subjecting the innocent to vexations which only the guilty deserve. These laws, whilst they make still worse the position of the assailed, improve that of their assailants; they increase rather than diminish the number of homicides, owing to the greater confidence with which an unarmed man may be attacked than an armed one. They are not so much preventive of crimes as fearful of them, due as they are to the excitement roused by particular facts, not to any reasoned consideration of the advantages or disadvantages of a general decree. Again, it is a false idea of utility, which would seek to impart to a multitude of intelligent beings the same symmetry and order that brute and inanimate matter admits of; which neglects present motives, the only constantly powerful influences with the generality of men, to give force to remote and future ones, the impression of which is very brief and feeble, unless a force of imagination beyond what is usual makes up, by its magnifying power, for the object's remoteness. Lastly, it is a false idea of utility, which, sacrificing the thing to the name, distinguishes the public good from that of every individual member of the public. There is this difference between the state of society and the state of nature, that in the latter a savage only commits injuries against others with a view to benefit himself, whilst in the former state men are sometimes moved by bad laws to injure others without any corresponding benefit to themselves. The tyrant casts fear and dread into the minds of his slaves, but they return by repercussion with all the greater force to torment his own breast. The more confined fear is in its range, so much the less dangerous is it to him who makes it the instrument of his happiness; but the more public it is and the larger the number of people it agitates, so much the more likely is it that there will be some rash, some desperate, or some clever and bold man who will try to make use of others for his own purpose, by raising in them hopes, that are all the more pleasant and seductive as the risk incurred in them is spread over a greater number, and as the value attached by the wretched to their existence diminishes in proportion to their misery. This is the reason why offences ever give rise to fresh ones: that hatred is a feeling much more durable than love, inasmuch as it derives its force from the very cause that weakens the latter, namely, from the continuance of the acts that produce it.

CHAPTER XXXIX

Of Family Spirit

Such fatal and legalised iniquities as have been referred to have been approved of by even the wisest men and practised by even the freest republics, owing to their having regarded society rather as an aggregate of families than as one of individuals. Suppose there to be 100,000 individuals, or 20,000 families, of five persons each, including its representative head: if the association is constituted by families, it will consist of 20,000 men and 80,000 slaves; if it be an association of individuals, it will consist of 100,000 citizens, and not a single slave. In the first case there will be a republic, formed of 20,000 little sovereignties; in the second the republican spirit will breathe, not only in the market-places and meetings of the people, but also within the domestic walls, wherein lies so great a part of human happiness or misery. In the first case, also, as laws and customs are the result of the habitual sentiments of the members of the republic—that is, of the heads of families—the monarchical spirit will gradually introduce itself, and its effects will only be checked by the conflicting interests of individuals, not by a feeling that breathes liberty and equality. Family spirit is a spirit of detail and confined to facts of trifling importance. But the spirit which regulates communities is master of general principles, overlooks the totality of facts, and combines them into kinds and classes, of importance to the welfare of the greater number. In the community of families sons remain in the power of the head of the family so long as he lives, and are obliged to look forward to his death for an existence dependent on the laws alone. Accustomed to submission and fear in the freshest and most vigorous time of life, when their feelings are less modified by that timidity, arising from experience, which men call moderation, how shall they withstand those obstacles in the way of virtue which vice ever opposes, in that feeble and failing period of life when despair of living to see the fruit of their labours hinders them from making vigorous changes?

When the community is one of individuals, the subordination that prevails in the family prevails by agreement, not by compulsion; and the sons, as soon as their age withdraws them from their state of natural dependence, arising from their feebleness and their need of education and protection, become free members of the domestic commonwealth, subjecting themselves to its head, in order to share in its advantages, as free men do by society at large. In the other condition the sons—that is, the largest and most useful part of a nation—are placed altogether at the mercy of their fathers; but in this one there is no enjoined connection between them, beyond that sacred and inviolable one of the natural ministration of necessary aid, and that of gratitude for benefits received, which is less often destroyed by the native wickedness of the human heart than by a law-ordained and ill-conceived state of subjection.

Such contradictions between the laws of a family and the fundamental laws of a State are a fertile source of other contradictions between public and private morality, giving rise consequently to a perpetual conflict in every individual mind. For whilst private morality inspires fear and subjection, public morality teaches courage and freedom; whilst the former inculcates the restriction of well-doing to a small number of persons indiscriminately, the latter inculcates its extension to all classes of men; and whilst the one enjoins the constant sacrifice of self to a vain idol, called 'the good of the family' (which is frequently not the good of any single member that composes it), the other teaches men to benefit themselves, provided they break not the laws, and incites them, by the reward of enthusiasm, which is the precursor of their action, to sacrifice themselves to the good of their country. Such contradictions make men scorn to follow virtue, which they find so complicated and confused, and at that distance from them, which objects, both moral and physical, derive from their obscurity. How often it happens that a man, in reflecting on his past actions, is astonished at finding himself dishonest. The larger society grows, the smaller fraction of the whole does each member of it become, and the more is the feeling of the commonwealth diminished, unless care be taken by the laws to reinforce it. Societies, like human bodies, have their circumscribed limits, extension beyond which involves inevitably a disturbance of their economy. The size of a State ought apparently to vary inversely with the sensibility of its component parts; otherwise, if both increase together, good laws will find, in the very benefit they have effected, an obstacle to the prevention of crimes. Too large a republic can only save itself from despotism by a process of subdivision, and a union of the parts into so many federative republics. But how effect this, save by a despotic dictator with the courage of Sylla and as much genius for construction as he had for destruction? If such a man be ambitious, the glory of all the ages awaits him; and if he be a philosopher, the blessings of his fellow-citizens will console him for the loss of his authority, even should he not become indifferent to their ingratitude. In proportion as the feelings which unite us to our own nation are weakened, do those for the objects immediately around us gain in strength; and it is for this reason that under the severest despotism the strongest friendships are to be found, and that the family virtues, ever of an exalted character, are either the most common or the only ones. It is evident, therefore, how limited have been the views of the great majority of legislators.

CHAPTER XL

Of The Treasury

There was a time when nearly all penalties were pecuniary. Men's crimes were the prince's patrimony; attempts against the public safety were an object of gain, and he whose function it was to defend it found his interest in seeing it assailed. The object of punishment was then a suit between the treasury, which exacted the penalty, and the criminal: it was a civil business, a private rather than a public dispute, which conferred upon the treasury other rights than those conferred upon it by the calls of the public defence, whilst it inflicted upon the offender other grievances than those he had incurred by the necessity of example. The judge was, therefore, an advocate for the treasury rather than an impartial investigator of the truth, an agent for the Chancellor of the Exchequer rather than the protector and minister of the laws. But as in this system to confess a fault was the same thing as to confess oneself a debtor to the treasury, that being the object of the criminal procedure in those days, so the confession of a crime, and a confession so managed as to favour and not to hurt fiscal interests, became and still remains (effects always outlasting their causes so long) the centre point of all criminal procedure. Without such confession a criminal convicted by indubitable proofs will incur a penalty less than the one legally attached to his crime; and without it he will escape torture for other crimes of the same sort which he may have committed. With it, on the other hand, the judge becomes master of a criminal's person, to lacerate him by method and formality, in order to get from him as from so much stock all the profit he can. Given the fact of the crime as proved, confession affords a convincing proof; and, to make this proof still less open to doubt, it is forcibly exacted by the agonies and despair of physical pain; whilst at the same time a confession that is extra-judicial, that is tendered calmly and indifferently, and without the overpowering fears of a trial by torture, is held insufficient for a verdict of guilt. Inquiries and proofs, which throw light upon the fact, but which weaken the claims of the treasury, are excluded; nor is it out of consideration for his wretchedness and weakness that a criminal is sometimes spared from torture, but out of regard for the claims which this entity, now mythical and inconceivable, might lose. The judge becomes the enemy of the accused, who stands in chains before him, the prey of misery, of torments, and the most terrible future; he does not seek to find the truth of a fact, but to find the crime in the prisoner, trying to entrap him, and thinking it to the loss of his own credit if he fail to do so, and to the detriment of that infallibility which men pretend to possess about everything. The evidence that justifies a man's imprisonment rests with the judge; in order that a man may prove himself innocent, he must first be declared guilty: that is called an *offensive prosecution*; and such are criminal proceedings in nearly every part of enlightened Europe, in the eighteenth century. The real prosecution, the *informative* one—that is, the indifferent inquiry into a fact, such as reason enjoins, such as military codes employ, and such as is used even by Asiatic despotism in trivial and unimportant cases—is of very scant use in the tribunals of Europe. What a complex maze of strange absurdities, doubtless incredible to a more fortunate posterity! Only the philosophers of that time will read in the nature of man the possible actuality of such a system as now exists.

CHAPTER XLI

The Prevention Of Crimes—Of Knowledge—Magistrates—Rewards—Education

It is better to prevent crimes than to punish them. This is the chief aim of every good system of legislation, which is the art of leading men to the greatest possible happiness or to the least possible misery, according to calculation of all the goods and evils of life. But the means hitherto employed for this end are for the most part false and contrary to the end proposed. It is impossible to reduce the turbulent activity of men to a geometrical harmony without any irregularity or confusion. As the constant and most simple laws of nature do not prevent aberrations in the movements of the planets, so, in the infinite and contradictory attractions of pleasure and pain, disturbances and disorder cannot be prevented by human laws. Yet this is the chimera that narrow-minded men pursue, when they have power in their hands. To prohibit a number of indifferent acts is not to prevent the crimes that may arise from them, but it is to create new ones from them; it is to give capricious definitions of virtue and vice which are proclaimed as eternal and immutable in their nature. To what should we be reduced if everything had to be forbidden us which might tempt us to a crime? It would be necessary to deprive a man of the use of his senses. For one motive that drives men to commit a real crime there are a thousand that drive them to the commission of those indifferent acts which are called crimes by bad laws; and if the likelihood of crimes is proportioned to the number of motives to commit them, an increase of the field of crimes is an increase of the likelihood of their commission. The majority of laws are nothing but privileges, or a tribute paid by all to the convenience of some few.

Would you prevent crimes, then cause the laws to be clear and simple, bring the whole force of a nation to bear on their defence, and suffer no part of it to be busied in overthrowing them. Make the laws to favour not so much classes of men as men themselves. Cause men to fear the laws and the laws alone. Salutary is the fear of the law, but fatal and fertile in crime is the fear of one man of another. Men as slaves are more sensual, more immoral, more cruel than free men; and, whilst the latter give their minds to the sciences or to the interests of their country, setting great objects before them as their model, the former, contented with the passing day, seek in the excitement of libertinage a distraction from the nothingness of their existence, and, accustomed to an uncertainty of result in everything, they look upon the result of their crimes as uncertain too, and so decide in favour of the passion that tempts them. If uncertainty of the laws affects a nation, rendered indolent by its climate, its indolence and stupidity is thereby maintained and increased; if it affects a nation, which though fond of pleasure is also full of energy, it wastes that energy in a number of petty cabals and intrigues, which spread distrust in every heart, and make treachery and dissimulation the foundation of prudence; if, again, it affects a courageous and brave nation, the uncertainty is ultimately destroyed, after many oscillations from liberty to servitude, and from servitude back again to liberty.

Would you prevent crimes, then see that enlightenment accompanies liberty. The evils that flow from knowledge are in inverse ratio to its diffusion; the benefits directly proportioned to it. A bold impostor, who is never a commonplace man, is adored by an ignorant people, despised by an enlightened one. Knowledge, by facilitating comparisons between objects and multiplying men's points of view, brings many different notions into contrast, causing them to modify one another, all the more easily as the same views and the same difficulties are observed in others. In the face of a widely diffused national enlightenment the calumnies of ignorance are silent, and authority, disarmed of pretexts for its manifestation, trembles; whilst the rigorous force of the laws remains unshaken, no one of education having any dislike to the clear and useful public compacts which secure the common safety, when he compares the trifling and useless liberty sacrificed by himself with the sum-total of all the liberties sacrificed by others, who without the laws might have been hostile to himself. Whoever has a sensitive soul, when he contemplates a code of well-made laws, and finds that he has only lost the pernicious liberty of injuring others, will feel himself constrained to bless the throne and the monarch that sits upon it.

It is not true that the sciences have always been injurious to mankind; when they were so, it was an inevitable evil. The multiplication of the human race over the face of the earth introduced war, the ruder arts, and the first laws, mere temporary agreements which perished with the necessity that gave rise to them. This was mankind's primitive philosophy, the few elements of which were just, because the indolence and slight wisdom of their framers preserved them from error. But with the multiplication of men there went ever a multiplication of their wants. Stronger and more lasting impressions were, therefore, needed, in order to turn them back from repeated lapses to that primitive state of disunion which each return to it rendered worse. Those primitive delusions, therefore, which peopled the earth with false divinities and created an invisible universe that governed our own, conferred a great benefit—I mean a great political benefit—upon humanity. Those men were benefactors of their kind, who dared to deceive them and drag them, docile and ignorant, to worship at the altars. By presenting to them objects that lay beyond the scope of sense and fled from their grasp the nearer they seemed to approach them—never despised, because never well understood—they concentrated their divided passions upon a single object of supreme interest to them. These were the first steps of all the nations that formed themselves out of savage tribes; this was the epoch when larger communities were formed, and such was their necessary and perhaps their only bond. I say nothing of that chosen people of God, for whom the most extraordinary miracles and the most signal favours were a substitute for human policy. But as it is the quality of error to fall into infinite subdivisions, so the sciences that grew out of it made of mankind a blind fanatical multitude, which, shut up within a close labyrinth, collides together in such confusion, that some sensitive and philosophical minds have regretted to this day the ancient savage state. That is the first epoch in which the sciences or rather opinions are injurious.

The second epoch of history consists in the hard and terrible transition from errors to truth, from the darkness of ignorance to the light. The great clash between the errors which are serviceable to a few men of power and the truths which are serviceable to the weak and the many, and the contact and fermentation of the passions at such a period aroused, are a source of infinite evils to unhappy humanity. Whoever ponders on the different histories of the world, which after certain intervals of time are so much alike in their principal episodes, will therein frequently observe the sacrifice of a whole generation to the welfare of succeeding ones, in the painful but necessary transition from the darkness of ignorance to the light of philosophy, and from despotism to freedom, which result from the sacrifice. But when truth, whose progress at first is slow and afterwards rapid (after men's minds have calmed down and the fire is quenched that purged a nation of the evils it suffered), sits as the companion of kings upon the throne, and is reverenced and worshipped in the parliaments of free governments, who will ever dare assert that the light which enlightens the people is more injurious than darkness, and that acknowledging the true and simple relations of things is pernicious to mankind?

If blind ignorance is less pernicious than confused half-knowledge, since the latter adds to the evils of ignorance those of error, which is unavoidable in a narrow view of the limits of truth, the most precious gift that a sovereign can make to himself or to his people is an enlightened man as the trustee and guardian of the sacred laws. Accustomed to see the truth and not to fear it; independent for the most part of the demands of reputation, which are never completely satisfied and put most men's virtue to a trial; used to consider humanity from higher points of view; such a man regards his own nation as a family of men and of brothers, and the distance between the nobles and the people seems to him so much the less as he has before his mind the larger total of the whole human species. Philosophers acquire wants and interests unknown to the generality of men, but that one above all others, of not belying in public the principles they have taught in obscurity, and they gain the habit of loving the truth for its own sake. A selection of such men makes the happiness of a people, but a happiness which is only transitory, unless good laws so increase their number as to lessen the probability, always considerable, of an unfortunate choice.

Another way of preventing crimes is to interest the magistrates who carry out the laws in seeking rather to preserve than to corrupt them. The greater the number of men who compose the magistracy, the less danger will there be of their exercising any undue power over the laws; for venality is more difficult among men who are under the close observation of one another, and their inducement to increase their individual authority diminishes in proportion to the smallness of the share of it that can fall to each of them, especially when they compare it with the risk of the attempt. If the sovereign accustoms his subjects, by formalities and pomp, by severe edicts, and by refusal to hear the grievances, whether just or unjust, of the man who thinks himself oppressed, to fear rather the magistrates than the laws, it will be more to the profit of the magistrates than to the gain of private and public security.

Another way to prevent crimes is to reward virtue. On this head I notice a general silence in the laws of all nations to this day. If prizes offered by academies to the discoverers of useful truths have caused the multiplication of knowledge and of good books, why should not virtuous actions also be multiplied, by prizes distributed from the munificence of the sovereign? The money of honour ever remains unexhausted and fruitful in the hands of the legislator who wisely distributes it.

Lastly, the surest but most difficult means of preventing crimes is to improve education—a subject too vast for present discussion, and lying beyond the limits of my treatise; a subject, I will also say, too intimately connected with the nature of government for it ever to be aught but a barren field, only cultivated here and there by a few philosophers, down to the remotest ages of public prosperity. A great man, who enlightens the humanity that persecutes him, has shown in detail the chief educational maxims of real utility to mankind; namely, that it consists less in a barren multiplicity of subjects than in their choice selection; in substituting originals for copies in the moral as in the physical phenomena presented by chance or intention to the fresh minds of youth; in inclining them to virtue by the easy path of feeling; and in deterring them from evil by the sure path of necessity and disadvantage, not by the uncertain method of command, which never obtains more than a simulated and transitory obedience.

CHAPTER XLII

Conclusion

From all that has gone before a general theorem may be deduced, of great utility, though little comformable to custom, that common lawgiver of nations. The theorem is this: 'In order that every punishment may not be an act of violence, committed by one man or by many against a single individual, it ought to be above all things public, speedy, necessary, the least possible in the given circumstances, proportioned to its crime, dictated by the laws.'

www.ingramcontent.com/pod-product-compliance
Lightning Source LLC
Chambersburg PA
CBHW031349230926
51848CB00002B/442
* 9 7 8 9 3 5 5 2 7 8 2 4 1 *